MTTC

Reading Specialist Practice Questions

I0877313

Mometrix
TEST PREPARATION

Dear Future Exam Success Story

First of all, **THANK YOU** for purchasing Mometrix study materials!

Second, congratulations! You are one of the few determined test-takers who are committed to doing whatever it takes to excel on your exam. **You have come to the right place.** We developed these practice tests with one goal in mind: to deliver you the best possible approximation of the questions you will see on test day.

Standardized testing is one of the biggest obstacles on your road to success, which only increases the importance of doing well in the high-pressure, high-stakes environment of test day. Your results on this test could have a significant impact on your future, and these practice tests will give you the repetitions you need to build your familiarity and confidence with the test content and format to help you achieve your full potential on test day.

Your success is our success

We would love to hear from you! If you would like to share the story of your exam success or if you have any questions or comments in regard to our products, please contact us at **800-673-8175** or **support@mometrix.com**.

Thanks again for your business and we wish you continued success!

Sincerely,
The Mometrix Test Preparation Team

Printed in the United States of America

Table of Contents

Practice Test #1

Multiple Choice Questions

1. Which of the following is LEAST accurate about ongoing informal assessments for English language Learners (ELLs)?

a. Ongoing informal assessments are able to demonstrate ELLs' content knowledge more validly than formal tests.
b. Ongoing informal assessments are usually more motivating for ELLs than formal tests.
c. Ongoing informal assessments are usually harder for ELLs to complete than formal tests.
d. Ongoing informal assessments provide the teacher with opportunity for more individualized instruction.

2. If a teacher were using a rubric to score the English language proficiency (ELP) of ELL students, which would best indicate that a student is at an intermediate level?

a. The student has mastered using basic grammar structures but not content vocabulary.
b. The student has mastered using content vocabulary but not basic grammar structures.
c. The student has mastered grammar basics despite some verb tense and number issues.
d. The student has mastered using both basic grammar structures and content vocabulary.

3. In a portfolio assessment, what content would be best for evaluating student skills in oral reading?

a. Student samples of compositions
b. Student audio recordings of stories
c. Student drawings depicting content
d. Student worksheets and filled forms

4. When screening or assessing student literacy development, what is a typical age or grade level for the stage of transitional literacy?

a. Toddlerhood
b. Preschool ages
c. In the first grade
d. Second/third grade

5. During assessment, a young child is able to identify and differentiate typical English-language speech sounds. This best reflects which type of awareness?

a. Phonic
b. Phonetic
c. Phonemic
d. Alphabetic

6. What should a young child NOT be able to identify during informal assessment of print concept awareness?

a. Where the teacher should start reading aloud
b. The title of the book
c. What a period means in a book
d. All of the words in the book

7. When assessing error patterns in a student's reading, which is most detrimental to reading proficiency?

a. Substitution of "control" for "contrariness"
b. Substitution of "resistant" for "recalcitrant"
c. Substituting a noun, not a verb, for a noun
d. Substituting for errors informed by context

8. During a reading assessment, which of the following student behaviors reflects a weakness in strategy?

a. The student tries to read every word, with many errors.
b. The student pays attention to the punctuation in a text.
c. The student understands the main idea, but not details.
d. The student takes a holistic approach to reading words.

9. A student participating in a reading assessment uses information from illustrations in the text he or she is reading to support reading performance. The student is using which kind of cue?

a. A visual cue
b. A meaning cue
c. A structural cue
d. A graphophonic cue

10. Assessment results often inform instructional practices. At what point should teachers begin teaching the stages of composition?

a. They should start teaching the stages of composition only after children have learned to form letters.
b. They should start teaching the stages of composition only after children have learned to spell words with reliable success.
c. They should start teaching the stages of composition only once children can generate full sentences.
d. They should start teaching the stages of composition concurrently as these writing skills develop.

11. Which instructional practice would NOT be helpful for young children to understand phonics and decode words?

a. Incidental exposure to implicit phonics in instruction
b. Systematic, explicit, and direct instruction in phonics
c. Teaching main ideas or strategic integration in reading activities
d. Giving reading and writing activities to apply phonics

12. Among study strategies that teachers can offer to help students, which ones belong in both the categories of summarizing strategies and knowledge management strategies?

a. Advance organizers and graphic organizers
b. Text-to-speech and speech-to-text software
c. Reading strategies like Multipass and SQ3R
d. Teaching main ideas or strategic integration

13. Compared with whole-class instruction, small-group instruction is particularly useful for which of the following?

a. Teach main ideas or strategic integration
b. Instruction in rhyming and onsets
c. Use read-alouds for oral practice
d. Diagnose reading difficulties and design reading interventions

14. In the tiered response to intervention (RTI) approach, what has US Department of Education research found to be a best practice for reading instruction?

a. Give all students assessment-based differentiated reading instruction in Tier 1.
b. Give all students the same reading instruction in Tier 1 and differentiate in Tier 2.
c. Give all students differentiated screening; differentiate based on results, not tiers.
d. Give all students the same reading instruction in Tiers 1 and 2, and differentiate in Tier 3.

15. When a teacher leading a reading center implements differentiated instruction, what is true about the parameters for small-group lessons?

a. Each small group should have an equal number of students.
b. The teacher uses the same lesson structure for each group.
c. The frequency and duration of attendance varies by group.
d. Instructional levels vary, but not the content in skills areas.

16. Regarding alternative lesson structures for differentiating reading instruction, for which of these should a teacher use skills-focused lessons rather than guided reading lessons?

a. For monitoring how well students apply skills to reading text
b. For helping students in mastering comprehension strategies
c. For helping students discuss the meaning of texts they read
d. For supporting students in using reading comprehension skills

17. As students progress in reading from primary to intermediate grade levels, how is small-group reading instruction best used with intermediate-grade readers?

a. For demonstrations
b. For interventions
c. For instruction on word meanings
d. For group responses to the same text or different texts

18. Within a comprehensive literacy program, which of the following descriptions most reflects the nature of small-group differentiated reading instruction?

a. Students have access to ongoing, direct teacher contact while interacting with peers.
b. The teaching and learning of literacy are accomplished through individual interaction.
c. The knowledge of literacy is accumulated through contributions from multiple voices.
d. Students accomplish their learning of literacy through completely independent work.

19. In LEAD21 reading instruction, which of these factors are differentiated?

a. Teacher expectations and student tasks
b. Text choices and teacher support levels
c. Teacher expectations and support levels
d. Text choices and student tasks assigned

20. Among grouping practices, which of the following have researchers found regarding whole-group instruction?

a. It can be the least efficient use of materials and time.
b. It can make it harder for students to tune out teaching.
c. It can lead to more active student lesson participation.
d. It can enable acceleration, given effective scaffolding.

21. Which of these best describes the "during reading" phase of whole-class reading instruction with a focus on decoding phonological patterns?

a. Partners reading a text together and help one another decode new words as they encounter them.
b. Teachers monitor student progress and provide assistance when necessary while independently reading through an assigned text.
c. Students read the text as partners and take turns reading and listening to one another.
d. Teachers read sentences aloud, demonstrating decoding practices. Students then repeat together as a class.

22. Practical instructional activities that develop student listening skills include which of the following?

a. Teaching students how to follow rather than give directions
b. Teaching students how to give rather than follow directions
c. Teaching students interpersonal communication skills
d. Teaching students to appreciate conversation, not oral literature

23. Which statement is correct about how teachers can model appropriate listening and speaking behaviors for students?

a. Teachers can model these when they facilitate book discussions, not in everyday conversations.
b. Teachers can model these better when giving whole-class instruction rather than small-group teaching.
c. Teachers can model these more authentically in one-to-one conversations than in discussions of media.
d. Teachers can model these and support them by thinking aloud about specific content they teach.

24. To teach students nonverbal communication skills, what have some teachers discovered through experience?

a. Nonverbal communication should be taught to students in large portions.
b. Nonverbal communication should be taught using appropriate situations.
c. Nonverbal communication does not require students to have confidence.
d. Nonverbal communication does not involve creativity from the students.

25. What is true about pre-production activities that teachers can use to encourage English-language speech by ELL students?

a. Narrating students' actions will simply make them self-conscious.
b. The activities that teachers use should involve hands-on learning.
c. It is more important that activities use speech than have meaning.
d. Language functions are irrelevant if students complete the lesson.

26. In an English language proficiency (ELP) standard for third-grade ELL students to apply standard English conventions in their speech, what is a key distinction among levels?

a. Pronunciation errors impeding communication are common only at the beginning level.
b. Grammatical errors interfere with communication only for the early intermediate level.
c. Habitual grammatical errors sometimes impede communication at the early advanced level.
d. Students no longer make grammatical errors once they have reached an advanced level.

27. What is true about speech or language delays and disorders?

a. Delays and disorders both involve abnormal language development sequences.
b. The only difference between delays and disorders is the severity of the problem.
c. Speech or language disorders are more common than speech or language delays.
d. Speech or language delays always involve slower language development rates.

28. A teacher initiates a guessing game to promote phonological awareness with first graders. The teacher presents picture cards and speaks each word depicted very slowly (e.g., "sssssuuuuunnnnn") to emphasize its phonemes, and children must guess the words. Which phonological process does this teach?

a. Blending phonemes
b. Deleting phonemes
c. Segmenting phonemes
d. Substituting phonemes

29. Which of the following is most accurate about the benefits of various levels of phonological awareness instruction to the development of reading skills?

a. Instruction in rhyming, onsets, and rimes appears most directly beneficial to reading development.
b. Instruction in simpler phonology skills can aid teaching more complex ones and reading development.
c. Instruction that integrates blending and segmenting appears most beneficial to reading development.
d. Instruction that integrates deleting and substituting appears most beneficial to reading development.

30. On a continuum, which of these represents the most complex level of phonological awareness?

a. Segmenting words into their individual syllables and blending individual syllables into words
b. Phonemic awareness, i.e., understanding words consist of phonemes and manipulating these
c. Segmenting words into their onsets and rimes and blending onsets and rimes into full words
d. Segmenting sentences, i.e., understanding speech consists of separate words, and rhyming songs

31. Regarding the relationship of phonemic awareness to reading and writing, which is NOT true?

a. Phonemic awareness is a listening and speaking skill, not a reading and writing skill.
b. Including print letters and words in teaching phonemic awareness is more effective.
c. Using print letters and words alone in teaching phonemic awareness is sufficient.
d. Pointing to printed letters while saying them aloud to draw attention to sound-letter connections is helpful.

32. What is an example of the phonemic awareness instructional strategy of keyword substitution?

a. "Show, show, show your shoat, shently…"
b. "How much is that window in the doggie"
c. "'Twas brillig, and the slithy toves / Did…"
d. "Owe, owe, owe our oat, ently own the…"

33. Which of these accurately reflects a guideline for teaching phonemic awareness based on the research literature?

a. Explicit instruction in phonemic awareness is found to be required for all students.
b. Instruction should be driven by analysis of data from phonemic awareness testing.
c. Instruction in phonemic awareness is more effective when phonemes are implicit.
d. Effective phonemic awareness instruction is scaffolded identically for all students.

34. Of the following, which is most correct in regard to children matching voice to print?

a. It is not normal for a second grader to finger-point to words when reading.
b. Giving young children creative, fun pointers is wrong, as these are crutches.
c. Older student finger-pointing shows reading struggles and impedes fluency.
d. Using bookmarks/popsicle sticks sideways has no effect on finger-pointing.

35. Which of these best reflects recommendations in instructional plans for teaching children the alphabetic principle?

a. Practice opportunities with cumulative review and new relationships
b. Explicitly teaching letter-sound correspondences in words to children
c. Special weekly opportunities to practice letter-sound correspondence
d. Opportunities to apply learning to unfamiliar, correctly spelled words

36. For students with problems retrieving or naming, which is the best instructional strategy to teach letter-sound associations?

a. Decoding closed-syllable, CVC words should begin after students master all consonant associations.
b. Decoding closed-syllable, CVC words should begin after students master all short vowel associations.
c. Decoding closed-syllable, CVC words should start after students master all consonants and one to two vowels.
d. Decoding closed-syllable, CVC words should begin once students master one to two short vowel sound-letter associations and several high-frequency sound-letter associations.

37. Among some of the critical components of good phonics lessons, which one is taught for the purpose of helping students to decode unfamiliar words?

a. Introducing sound-spellings
b. Blending phonemes into words
c. Discriminating phonemes in words
d. Reviewing to overlearn sound-spellings

38. In phonics instruction, what is accurate relative to phonological discrimination exercises?

a. Children's invented spellings may omit consonants, but never vowels.
b. Children can discriminate short vowels more easily than long vowels.
c. Children can discriminate long vowels more easily than short vowels.
d. Children must learn to discriminate short vowels before long vowels in words.

39. What has research found about systematic, explicit instruction in phonics?

a. Explicit instruction in phonics makes significant improvements in children's reading comprehension.
b. Explicit instruction in phonics makes significant improvements in K-1 word recognition, not spelling.
c. Explicit instruction in phonics makes significant improvements only for children with typical reading development.
d. Explicit instruction in phonics makes significant improvements as a whole language reading program for beginning readers.

40. Which of these applies the principle of teaching from simpler to more complex for instruction in decoding multisyllabic words?

a. Teaching open syllables first among syllable pattern types
b. Teaching closed syllables first among syllable pattern types
c. Teaching syllabication before introducing multisyllabic words
d. Teaching syllable patterns based upon spelling generalizations

41. A student is using cues in a text he or she is reading to construct meaning from it. Which of the following self-questions that the student asks indicates that the student is using graphophonic cues?

a. "Do all of these words, taken together, make sense?"
b. "Do these words, taken in this order, sound correct?"
c. "Do these new words' letter patterns match others?"
d. "Do all of these words look right to spell the sounds?"

42. A student incorrectly pronounces the word *rattle* with a long vowel *a*. The teacher explains a general rule to the student about splitting doubled consonants. This instructional strategy focuses most on using which of these?

a. Structural analysis
b. Spelling patterns
c. Syllabication
d. Morphemes

43. A student reading a text sees the word "sow" in a sentence. Which of the following will NOT help the student figure out the word meaning and pronunciation in this case?

a. The meaning of the surrounding sentence(s)
b. The sentence's syntax and grammatical structure
c. The dictionary definitions given for the word
d. The spelling pattern of the word

44. What is the *most* accurate statement about dictionaries relative to denotative and connotative word meanings?

a. Dictionaries only provide denotative meanings of words.
b. Dictionaries may offer examples of both types of meaning.
c. Dictionaries only offer connotative meanings for words.
d. Dictionary definitions differ from denotative meanings.

45. Which of these best identifies what developing automatic word recognition improves for students?

a. Recall quality and organization, via fluency and comprehension
b. Reading automaticity and speed, irrespective of comprehension
c. Reading comprehension, irrespective of how reading is recalled
d. Recall accuracy, organization, and detail irrespective of fluency

46. Using E. B. White's *Stuart Little* as an example, which response represents evaluative comprehension?

a. "Stuart Little, who is the main character in this story, is a mouse."
b. "Stuart's parents, Mr. and Mrs. Frederick C. Little, are humans."
c. "Stuart's size and doing things a mouse can do help his family."
d. "Stuart likes to be first up in the morning; I like to sleep late."

47. Researchers have found effective programs that promote independent reading share which common element(s)?

a. Active parental involvement is the one important element shared among all effective programs.
b. They focus on collaboration of other significant adults in students' lives rather than active parental involvement.
c. They all have access to varied material, community partnerships, parental involvement, and adult collaboration.
d. Partnerships among community institutions and access to varied material are the most important.

48. Which of these is accurate about instruction that supports independent, reflective student reading?

a. Students typically write in reader response journals after both sustained silent and independent reading.
b. Student journals enable teachers to monitor reading, check comprehension, discuss, and suggest books.
c. Students typically can write in reader response journals without any modeling, prompting, or references.
d. Students should be advised to achieve a balance of 50 percent reading and 50 percent writing.

49. Educational researchers have found which of the following literary genres most appropriate for improving reading comprehension in public schools?

a. Novels
b. Poems
c. Short stories
d. Drama (plays)

50. Which is least effective when instructing students in basic literary analysis skills that are arranged in a hierarchy of progressive difficulty (based on research results)?

a. Teachers should instruct one skill at a time to master before moving higher within the hierarchy.
b. Teachers should address every skill in the hierarchy without waiting for students to master them.
c. Teachers should frequently re-teach all skills throughout the year using progressively more complex materials.
d. Teachers should frequently evaluate students' skills throughout the year.

51. Among instructional strategies that aid in student comprehension of nonfictional text, which of these is most useful for promoting critical thinking?

a. Answering open-ended questions about texts
b. Skimming the text for features that give signs
c. Establishing connections between text and life
d. Establishing connections between text and self

52. Some teachers suggest a simple visual graphic to teach younger and beginning reading students about the main idea and supporting details in nonfiction text: outline your hand on the board and have students follow suit (or give them prepared handouts with a hand outline). Label parts of the hand. Where on the hand drawing would the supporting details logically be?

a. On the thumb of the hand
b. On the fingers of the hand
c. On the palm of the hand
d. On the back of the hand

53. Which of the following instructional strategies helps students ask questions about text, make predictions, and then read further to confirm or deny what they predicted?

a. Gist
b. DRTA
c. Fishbowl
d. Cornell Notes

54. Which of the following purposes for writing is most likely to be included within another?

a. Description within narration
b. Narration within description
c. Persuasion within exposition
d. Exposition within narration

55. Which of these describes a student action that is characteristic of recursive writing?

a. A student writes an introduction, then the body of a work, and finishes by writing a conclusion.
b. A student brainstorms, outlines, and writes; edits it once and turns it in; and discards it after it is graded.
c. A student inserts another excellent point that just occurred to her right before publishing.
d. A student follows the five stages of writing and editing exactly, always in the prescribed sequence.

56. Experts (Wallace et al., 2007) recommend instructional writing strategies for improving reading comprehension. Which one of these does this through helping students to see information from various perspectives?

a. Read, respond, revisit, discuss
b. Four square graphic organizer
c. About/point
d. Cubing

57. Researchers have identified five developmental stages of spelling. Which choice orders these stages in the correct sequence of development?

a. Derivational relations spelling, emergent spelling, letter name-alphabetic spelling, syllables and affixes spelling, within-word pattern spelling
b. Letter name-alphabetic spelling, syllables and affixes spelling, within-word pattern spelling, emergent spelling, derivational relations spelling
c. Emergent spelling, letter name-alphabetic spelling, within-word pattern spelling, syllables and affixes spelling, derivational relations spelling
d. Within-word pattern spelling, emergent spelling, derivational relations spelling, syllables and affixes spelling, letter name-alphabetic spelling

58. Among regular word spellings, which of these frequently recurring patterns is reflected by the spelling of *-tion* as the final syllable of many English nouns?

a. Reliable, but non-phonetic, patterns
b. Recurring phonetic spelling patterns
c. Etymological extensions to patterns
d. Spellings for Greek and Latin stems

59. To inform instructional strategies for writing mechanics, which of the following is an appropriate benchmark for students in grades 3-5?

a. Using periods after declarative sentences
b. Using question marks after interrogatives
c. Using commas to divide a series of words
d. Using quotation marks around quotations

60. A teacher familiarizes students with various kinds of information sources, how researchers use them, and specific conventions they follow. The teacher compares the merits, usefulness, relevance, and appropriateness of these sources relative to a class topic. How do students benefit from this instruction?

a. Direct learning about various types of source materials is the only benefit.
b. They gain deeper understanding and critical engagement via various perspectives.
c. How to build topic-related positions using evidence is not among benefits.
d. Students gain insight into selecting materials but not into evaluating them.

61. When teachers assign students to take research notes on sources they find and read, what do they also need to advise students to do?

a. To make more generalized notes rather than more detailed notes
b. To note both quotations and paraphrases without differentiating
c. To differentiate quoting, paraphrasing, and commentaries clearly
d. To note both their own paraphrases and commentaries the same

62. A teacher explains and models steps for fourth-grade students to follow in asking and answering research questions using text and text features. Which represents the most effective sequence for these steps?

a. Write research questions, use table of contents and headings in selected text to find information, read identified chapters for pertinent information, classify or categorize information by which question it answers
b. Use table of contents and headings in selected text to find information, read identified chapters for pertinent information, classify or categorize information by which question it answers, write research questions
c. Read identified chapters for pertinent information, write research questions, classify or categorize information by which question it answers, use table of contents and headings in selected text to find information
d. Classify or categorize information by which question it answers, use table of contents and headings in selected text to find information, write research questions, read identified chapters for pertinent information

63. Some teachers have integrated smartphones into school curriculum as a way of using available technology to support the learning and practice of student research. What is correct about this trend?

a. Smartphones are projected to become too expensive as teaching tools.
b. Teachers should allow students to use the resources that they have.
c. It is unnecessary for a school to create an acceptable use policy for this.
d. Teachers need to know how to get information from students' phones.

64. Of the following, which kind of learning disability would have the most direct impact on a student's reading instruction?

a. An expressive language disorder
b. A receptive language disorder
c. An articulation disorder
d. A movement disorder

65. Relative to the influences of cultural contexts on language development, which of these is true about various world cultures and languages?

a. All cultures have social conventions and body language as well as spoken, written, or signed language.
b. All cultures have spoken but not necessarily written language.
c. All cultures have written but not necessarily spoken language.
d. All cultures have only social conventions and body language.

66. According to recent research findings, diagnosed reading difficulties such as dyslexia are primarily ______ in origin.

a. Neurological and developmental
b. Environmental and ecological
c. Neurological and environmental
d. Developmental and environmental

67. Which of these is mainly a sign that a student has problems with reading comprehension?

a. The student has trouble recognizing words out of context.
b. The student reads laboriously, reading one word at a time.
c. The student has trouble separating the main idea from details.
d. The student has trouble relating a text to prior knowledge.

68. Research into instructional strategies for teaching sight words to students with moderate and severe intellectual disabilities has found which of the following?

a. Traditional approaches are effective for generalization.
b. Some orthographic approaches are better than others.
c. Classroom acquisition outpaces community acquisition.
d. Community-based instruction promotes generalization.

69. Which statement accurately reflects educational measurement principles relative to how teachers should design reading assessments?

a. Teachers should design tests to measure a small sample of their learning objectives.
b. Teachers should design tests to instruct as well as to diagnose or evaluate students.
c. Teachers should design tests to compare groups using criterion-referenced scoring.
d. Teachers should design tests to be either valid or reliable, as both are unnecessary.

70. Among the following, which is an indicator of reliability in a reading assessment instrument?

a. The test measures the reading skill it specifically claims to measure.
b. The test measures the reading skill through open-ended questions.
c. The test measures the reading skill using a few very focused items.
d. The test measures the reading skill consistently over repeated uses.

71. In investigating the best instructional strategies and tools for planning and implementing school reading programs, what have researchers found?

a. Explicit phonics instruction enables higher achievement only for at-risk students.
b. Instruction incorporating decodable books has been discredited by researchers.
c. Student use of word identification strategies is unrelated to what text they read.
d. Prior student literacy knowledge helps to develop sound-spelling understanding.

72. Research into professional development (PD) to instruct teachers in how to plan and implement effective research-based reading programs finds which main component 100 percent necessary for teachers to apply what they learn in their own classrooms?

a. Coaching
b. Practicing
c. Modeling
d. Feedback

73. Among practices for differentiating reading instruction, which of these represents a valid one?

a. Materials used for read-alouds should be for fun and not common teaching texts.
b. Teachers should instruct the whole class uniformly by using the same single text.
c. Teachers should reserve enough class time for students to read at comfort levels.
d. To reach all student reading levels, teachers should base each unit upon the text.

74. Which of these is most accurate about the failure of some reading curriculum designs?

a. Curriculum designs fail when their components fail, rather than being incompatible.
b. An essential element of curriculum design is provision for continuous improvement.
c. Curriculum designs fail due to component incompatibility, not to component failure.
d. Personnel not wanting to implement or misunderstanding a design cause its failure.

75. In describing a literacy-rich learning environment for younger students, what is most correct?

a. Labeling everything in the classroom only distracts the attention of the youngest students.
b. Directions, calendars, signs, and schedules are organizational tools not supporting literacy.
c. Word and picture labels should be avoided for discriminating against the visually impaired.
d. Students experience lessons directly if they and teachers redo classrooms as themes or texts.

76. According to the National Education Association (NEA, 2011), one main strategy for effective family-community partnerships is for all members to agree about core values. What accurately describes another strategy for engaging stakeholders?

a. School personnel use community priorities as bases to develop action plans on their own.
b. Schools provide data-based on-site professional development for teachers to collaborate.
c. Schools scrutinize data to examine achievement trends and address student areas of need.
d. Schools accept community partnership offers as a bonus instead of recruiting strategically.

77. Which of these have researchers found about the relationship of family involvement in education to student outcomes?

a. Students with families involved in their learning get higher grades, take more advanced classes, have higher graduation rates, and are more likely to attend postsecondary education.
b. Students perform their best academically when their parents concentrate on adopting one specific major role in their learning, like participating in school events and activities.
c. Students whose families actively support their learning have better attendance and attitudes toward school, but do not demonstrate any better behavior while they are there.
d. Students from diverse backgrounds feel more comfortable in school as a result of school-family collaboration to bridge cultural gaps, but are not found to perform better academically.

78. Among national recommendations for promoting family educational involvement at the school district level, which of these is an accurate representation?

a. Addressing diverse family needs systemically includes providing interpreting or translating services.
b. Supporting wrap-around community services is for meeting student academic, not other, needs.
c. Supporting district-wide policies promoting partnerships excludes the commitment of resources.
d. District collaborative work on policies and practices should give equal priority for all school sites.

79. Which statement is most accurate about the role of a facilitator during consensus-building meetings with stakeholders to discuss reading program issues?

a. The facilitator should always be one of those stakeholders.
b. The facilitator should always be a trained, skilled outsider.
c. The facilitator should always be neutral, and like a referee.
d. The facilitator should always further his or her own interests.

80. Relative to stakeholder concerns with a school reading program, what is true about conflict resolution?

a. Conflict is always negative; thus, it can and should be avoided.
b. Conflict resolution processes are unrelated to self-knowledge.
c. Conflict is an opportunity for social change and moral growth.
d. Conflict is ubiquitous, yet it is analyzed more but described less.

Constructed Response

1. Suppose that you are a reading specialist at a public middle school that has just received funding specifically for improving its infrastructure, equipment, and software to integrate technology into instruction. The principal asks you to design reading curriculum incorporating the technology.

- Summarize a reading lesson from this new curriculum wherein students use computers to complete the lesson and a short assignment interactively. Identify the learning objective(s) for this lesson.
- Identify and explain several of the advantages that this computer-assisted instruction will offer to the school's reading program.

2. Scenario: You are a reading specialist in a public middle school. A teacher refers Marco, a student in the eighth grade, for evaluation of his literacy skills and strategies. The teacher reports that Marco demonstrates advanced knowledge of vocabulary above grade level, acquires new words and meanings very easily, and enjoys learning new words across all subjects. The teacher also reports that Marco seems to have great difficulty summarizing reading in the correct sequence, whether chronological, logical, etc. He has no trouble retaining information but does have trouble with sorting it, outlining it, and sometimes with separating major points from minor details. The teacher would also like some suggestions from you for instructional strategies that will build on his literacy strengths and address his literacy needs.

Document 1 is a reading passage that you use in an informal assessment to evaluate Marco's reading comprehension. After he reads it silently for the first time, you ask him questions about the material. He scores 100 percent on questions about word meanings and 89 percent on comprehension questions. When asked to summarize the main points of the passage in their order of occurrence, he scores 30 percent.

Use the information from this scenario and the documents below to write a response addressing these two tasks:

a. Identify and describe one area of literacy strength and one area of literacy need that Marco demonstrates. Support your identifications and descriptions by citing evidence in the scenario and the documents provided.

b. For the area of literacy need you identified in the previous task, identify and describe one instructional strategy that you can suggest for the teacher to address it, while also building on the area of literacy strength you previously identified.

DOCUMENT 1:

Reading Passage for Informal Assessment

"Sometimes when we look at it, it looks crazy," remarked Adam Steltzner, an engineer who works for the National Aeronautics and Space Administration—more commonly known to the world as NASA. "It is the result of reasoned engineering thought. But it still looks crazy."

In a video story entitled "Seven Minutes of Terror," Steltzner was joined on camera by an eloquent cast of entry-descent-landing engineers (or "EDL engineers"). Working from the Jet Propulsion Laboratory (JPL) in California, their team introduced the world to one of the most daring, inventive feats of engineering the world had ever witnessed: the pinpoint landing of NASA's Curiosity rover on Mars.

The seven minutes explored in that story—and experienced by the world in early August 2012—took place after seven years of engineering, one year of space flight, and countless hours of collaboration on the perfect landing. Dubbed the Mars Science Laboratory ("MSL"), this mission brought together more than 7,000 people, working in organizations from all over the world, to accomplish its goals. Split into two parts, the launch and the landing, MSL is one of the greatest technological accomplishments of human history.

(© ReadWorks, Inc., 2013)

DOCUMENT 2:

Teacher's Anecdotal Record

10/22: Marco read through a text assignment fairly quickly. After reading, he was able to give correct definitions for all target vocabulary words. When asked to make an outline of the text he read, Marco was unable to classify its points into headings and subheadings.

11/12: Marco scored 100 percent on both the spelling test for this week and a cumulative vocabulary test covering the past month's science lessons. His scores are the same for spelling and vocabulary in other subject areas.

11/15: In an oral formative assessment, I asked Marco to summarize the social studies text he had just read. He was able to identify several of the most important ideas, but he put them in the wrong logical sequence. He also identified the events described in the text out of chronological order.

12/12: I gave a class assignment to write an essay on an earth and space science topic. Students could choose from a list of topics related to what we covered in this unit. Marco found the subject matter interesting and had no trouble choosing his preferred topic. He did not make an outline before starting to write, as he found this too difficult. (See note from 10/22.) I suggested he at least make a list of ideas, points, or subtopics, which he did.

12/15: In the essay I assigned on 12/12, Marco included plenty of pertinent information but without any apparent structure. He had difficulty paragraphing. First, he wrote everything in one long paragraph. Then, when I prompted him, he tried dividing his writing into paragraphs, but the divisions did not correspond to the subject matter.

Answer Key and Explanations for Test #1

Multiple Choice Questions

1. C: Ongoing informal assessments include any actions the teacher takes to check for students' comprehension of the material, even so small as to ask for classroom discussion about a story to gauge how well the class as a whole understands the content. Because ongoing informal assessments are so casual, they tend to be faster and easier for all students to complete, and the students may be unaware that they are even being assessed. This lack of pressure, combined with the opportunity to ask questions tailored to individual student, gives the teacher a great opportunity to assess, provide individualized instruction, and motivate students at the same time.

Informal assessments tend to better reflect an English language learner's (ELL) content knowledge than formal tests because formal tests present several issues with testing reliability and validity and may not accurately gauge content knowledge alone. For instance, a science or mathematics test may not present any linguistic difficulties to a native English speaker, and will not interfere with the test's ability to gauge their content knowledge. For an ELL, however, a student may encounter linguistic barriers that interfere with their comprehension or speed in taking a test and consequently interferes with the accurate measurement of their understanding of the subject matter.

Informal assessments do tend to hold lower weight in grades than formal tests because they are too individualized and casual to provide a full picture of progress toward comprehension of the curriculum. Despite this, informal assessments are arguably more important than formal assessments because they are so effective for making flexible adjustments to instruction to better meet the needs of the student and the class as a whole.

2. C: An ELL student at the intermediate ELP has not completely mastered all basic grammatical structures or all content vocabulary. Students at intermediate levels will still demonstrate some difficulties with things like verb tense, number, and using content vocabulary. Students demonstrating mastery of both basic grammar structures and content vocabulary would be scored at an advanced rather than intermediate level using a rubric.

3. B: Student composition samples (A) and worksheets and forms that students have completed (D) are better portfolio content for evaluating student skills in writing. Student drawings depicting content (C) are better for evaluating student content knowledge. Audio recordings of students reading stories (B) are best for evaluating student skills in oral reading.

4. D: Toddlers (A), like infants, are in the first stage of literacy development, wherein they become aware of and explore environmental language. Preschoolers (B) experiment with early forms of reading and writing in the second stage. First-graders (C) typically attain early formal literacy learning in the third stage of development. By the second and third grades (D), students typically begin reading independently in the fourth stage, transitional literacy.

5. C: Phonic awareness, or phonics (A), is knowing how alphabet letters correspond to speech sounds and vice versa. Awareness of phonetics (B) is knowing specific individual variations in speech sounds within a language. Phonemic (C) awareness is knowing the standard, general, or typical speech sounds used in a language. Alphabetic (D) awareness is knowing the written letter symbols representing speech sounds. (The alphabetic principle is the basis of phonics.)

6. D: During informal assessment for print concept awareness, a young child who cannot read yet should be able to identify where the teacher would start reading the book aloud (A), the title of the book (B), the meaning of a period as the end of a sentence in the book (C), a word in or on the book as well as a letter within a word in the book and spaces between words in the book, and the front, back, and directionality of the book.

7. A: The type or pattern of error most damaging to reading proficiency is substituting words with similar appearances or spelling but completely different meanings, because this shows a lack of reading for meaning. Substituting synonyms (B) shows some comprehension of word meaning. Substituting like parts of speech (C) shows some comprehension of grammar and syntax. Substituting correct words or closer approximations for errors based on information from the sentence context (D) shows skills in both reading for meaning and self-correction.

8. D: Making at least the attempt to read every single word, even with many errors (A), is a strategic strength that gives students decoding practice and, even without success every time, enables their potential. Attending to punctuation in text (B) is a strength, since punctuation can significantly affect meaning (e.g., "Let's eat, Grandma" vs. "Let's eat Grandma"). Even without understanding all details, getting the gist of text meaning (C) is also a strength. However, holistic word reading (D) misses plural or verb tense endings and other morphological changes affecting meaning, reflecting a strategic weakness.

9. B: Although the illustrations themselves are visual images, using the information available from them to inform reading is not using a visual cue (A). Word appearance and length, familiar-looking phrases, and word-initial letters or phonemes—i.e., visual aspects of the verbal text itself—are examples of visual cues. Because the student uses information from illustrations, he or she uses a meaning cue (B). A structural cue (C) would involve using knowledge of syntax (sentence structure) to inform correct reading. A graphophonic cue (D) would involve using knowledge of sound-to-letter correspondences.

10. D: Teachers should instruct children in the stages of composition at the same time they are developing skills for forming letters (A), spelling words (B), and generating sentences (C) rather than waiting until after they have developed them. The multifaceted approach allows for more practice in all skills and can help reduce overloading instruction into just one element of language development.

11. C: Of the options, teaching main ideas or strategic integration of ideas refer more to reading comprehension than to phonics and decoding. The best option given is choice B, systematic, explicit, and direct instruction in phonics, as phonics is not as much of an acquired language skill as it is a taught language skill. Explicit instruction in early phonics instruction is most effective. As a child becomes more fluent, increased incidental exposure (choice A) can help to improve fluency in decoding skills. Choice D represents a blended activity, using features of both explicit and implicit instruction and should prove effective in helping students understand phonics and decode words.

12. A: Advance organizers and graphic organizers can be categorized as both summarizing and knowledge management strategies. Text-to-speech and speech-to-text software (B) belong in the category of adaptive materials, for special-needs students. Reading comprehension strategies like Multipass and SQ3R, which stands for Survey, Question, Read, Recite, and Review (C), belong in the category of self-questioning strategies. Teaching main ideas or strategic integration (D) belongs in the category of summarizing strategies, but not knowledge management strategies.

13. D: Teachers can much more easily diagnose specific reading difficulties in a few students at a time within a small group than in a whole class. Small-group instruction also makes it easier to design interventions for several students on similar reading levels with similar problem areas within a small group than for all students in a large class.

14. A: The federal Department of Education (ED)'s What Works Clearinghouse (WWC) finds the most effective practice in RTI is to give all students differentiated reading instruction in Tier 1 rather than only in Tier 2 (B) or Tier 3 (D). Although differentiating assessment is as important as differentiating instruction for many students, and it is important to differentiate based on assessment results, universally screening all students and differentiating instruction for all students in Tier 1 are equally important WWC recommendations for RTI, making choice C incorrect.

15. C: Small-group differentiated instruction in teacher-led reading centers typically uses flexible groups, varying group size (A) according to student need (e.g., five to seven students for good or average readers and three to five students for struggling readers). Teachers may use guided reading, a skills-focused lesson, or some other lesson structure depending on the group (B). Each group might attend for different durations (e.g., 10/20/30 minutes, etc.) and at different frequencies (e.g., twice weekly, three times per week, daily, etc.) as needed (C). The teacher varies the instructional levels and areas of focus in reading skills according to each group's needs (D).

16. B: A teacher should use guided reading lessons, not skills-focused lessons, to monitor how well students are applying the skills they have learned to reading text (A). Guided reading lessons are not the best format for helping students master comprehension strategies (B), phonics knowledge, phonemic decoding strategies, key vocabulary, or other fundamental reading skills if students have basic knowledge gaps in these. Skills-focused lessons are more effective to develop these skills before students can apply them to read for and discuss text meanings (C) with teacher support (D).

17. D: According to Wright Group (McGraw-Hill), authors of the LEAD21 model of small group reading instruction (SGRI), the purpose of SGRI in primary grades is more for teacher modeling and demonstration of reading skills through explicit instruction, whereas by the intermediate grades, through student progress the purpose has shifted more to student demonstration of shared responses to the same text and shared responses across different texts.

18. A: Small-group differentiated reading instruction allows students to interact with their peers while also having access to ongoing direct contact with their teacher. When literacy teaching and learning are accomplished through individual interaction (B), this reflects one-to-one reading instruction or intensive individualized intervention. When literacy knowledge is accumulated through contributions from multiple voices (C), this reflects whole-class or large-group instruction. While students may read independently and conduct independent study projects, they should still have some related interaction with their teacher (D).

19. B: In LEAD21 (Wright Group, McGraw-Hill) reading instruction, teacher expectations, and student tasks are kept uniform across all students, while the choices of texts and the levels of teacher support (B) are differentiated.

20. D: Researchers have found whole-group instruction often uses materials and time most efficiently. However, it is also most easily tuned out by students (B), frequently by those needing the most help, and allows greater student passivity (C). Solutions include intensifying classroom routines to be more useful for more students. Although whole-group assignment of the same text is harder for students reading below grade level, research finds difficult texts can accelerate their reading development, given effective teacher scaffolding (D).

21. D: Teacher-directed reading is one method of instructing the whole class together. In this method, the teacher often has a passage or patterned sentences that the teacher will use to model reading practices to the class. In the "pre-reading" phase, the teacher should give the students supportive information, such as the title, topic, or new key words that the student will encounter. In the "during reading" phase, the teacher will model a sentence, then ask the class to repeat the sentence, following along with the modeled decoding and tracking techniques. In the "after reading" phase, the teacher should ask the students to apply and practice this pattern more independently on their own to gain experience decoding and tracking. In this method, the "during reading" phase takes place actively as a class, which is not represented by the other choices. Independent or partner practice usually takes place in the "after reading" phase of this type of activity.

22. C: Practical instructional activities that develop student listening skills (cf. Wolvin and Coakley, 1979) include teaching students both to follow and give directions, teaching them interpersonal communication skills, and teaching them to appreciate oral literature.

23. D: According to experts, teachers can model appropriate listening and speaking behaviors for students when they facilitate book discussions and during everyday conversations with them (A), when giving instruction to both whole classes and small groups (B), in one-to-one conversations they have with students and during classroom media discussions (C), and by thinking aloud specifically about the content they are teaching (D).

24. B: Educational research into teaching practices for nonverbal communication is notably lacking; however, teachers who have experimented with lessons (cf. Darn, 2014) have discovered it is best to teach nonverbal communication skills in small chunks (A), using appropriate situations (B) wherein the context of the theme or situation is congruent with the language. They also find that to help students use gestures and expressions to reinforce linguistic meaning, teachers must include drama-based instructional activities that build student confidence (C) and creativity (D).

25. B: Experts find that narrating ELL students' actions, i.e., linguistic encoding, helps encourage them to speak English (A), that teachers should assign activities that include hands-on learning (B), and that the activities they assign should be meaningful (C). They also find that teachers should focus on which language function the students must apply to complete a lesson, not just that they complete it (D).

26. A: Typical state and district ELP standards for third-grade ELL students in applying standard English conventions in speech identify pronunciation errors as impeding communication at the beginning level, whereas only grammatical and structural errors interfere at the other levels. Multiple grammatical errors impede communication often at the early intermediate level, and habitual grammatical errors sometimes impede communication at the intermediate level (B). Some errors occur, but do not impede communication, at the early advanced level (C). At the advanced level, third-grade ELLs still make grammatical errors occasionally (D).

27. D: Speech or language delays and disorders always involve slower language development rates, but not always in the same ways. Speech or language delays involve a normal *sequence* of language development (A) but at slower rates than normal. Speech or language disorders involve abnormal language development, including development not following the normal sequence. Due to the broken sequence, language development is considered slow as disordered speech prevents children from hitting the appropriate benchmarks on time. Thus, severity is not the only difference (B). Speech or language delays are more common than speech or language disorders, not vice versa (C). In fact, speech or language delays are the most common developmental issue, affecting 5-10 percent of preschoolers.

28. A: The "guess the word" game described teaches the phonological process of blending phonemes, i.e., combining individual speech sounds into whole words. Deleting phonemes (B) would involve having students change words by removing one speech sound from each word to create a new one, e.g., from "brat" to "bat." Segmenting phonemes (C) would involve separating words into their individual component phonemes, e.g., "sun" to "s," "u," and "n." Substituting phonemes (D) would involve changing words by replacing one phoneme in each word with another, e.g., from "sun" to "fun."

29. C: Researchers have found that instruction in simpler phonological skills like rhyming, onsets, and rimes may not have any direct benefits for reading development (A); however, they find that teaching these simpler skills first nevertheless can make it easier to teach the more complex ones *without* directly benefiting reading development (B). Researchers have also found that the phonological awareness instruction that appears most beneficial to subsequent reading development integrates blending and segmenting (C), not deleting and substituting (D).

30. B: On a continuum, the simplest level of phonological awareness is represented by being able to recognize and produce rhymes in songs, and show understanding that sentences contain individual words by segmenting them (D). Segmenting words into syllables and blending syllables into words (A) represents a more complex level around the middle of the continuum. A higher level of complexity is segmenting words into onsets and rimes and blending onsets and rimes into words (C). The highest level is phonemic awareness, i.e., understanding that words contain individual phonemes and being able to manipulate (blend, segment, delete, substitute) these (B).

31. C: While it is true that phonemic awareness is a listening and speaking skill rather than a reading and writing skill (A), it is equally true that children develop phonemic awareness better when instruction combines print with speech sounds (B). This helps children realize how speech sounds and printed letters connect and apply this insight. However, just including print is not sufficient (C). Teachers should also point to printed letters while saying them aloud to draw children's attention to sound-letter connections (D).

32. A: Keyword substitution involves replacing a phoneme in key words of song lyrics or other common phrases and sayings. This gives children practice in wordplay and is entertaining. After singing the revised lyrics, teachers can discuss with children how changing one phoneme changed the meanings of words in the song. Changing /r/ to /ʃ/ in "Row, row, row your boat" (A) is an example. Choice B transposes the two nouns in the lyric. Keyword substitution refers to substituting different phonemes in key words, not substituting different whole words or transposing existing words. Choice C quotes the first line of Lewis Carroll's poem "Jabberwocky," famous for using many nonsense words. Choice D uses the same song as choice A but deletes initial phonemes rather than substituting.

33. B: Based on the research literature, guidelines for phonemic awareness instruction include using analysis of data from phonemic awareness assessments to drive instruction, because only a minority of students requires explicit instruction in phonemic awareness (A). However, effective instruction in phonemic awareness does explicitly label phonemes (C), as well as demonstrates phoneme blending and segmenting processes. Effective phonemic awareness instruction is also differentiated to account for individual differences, including various levels of scaffolding for different students (D).

34. C: Finger-pointing is normal for beginning readers, even into second grade (A); adults should not interfere with pointing. Giving young children "witch fingers," feathers, and other available, recycled, or homemade pointers is fine. These are not crutches (B); they are simply finger substitutes that are creative, fun, and keep book pages clean with younger readers. However, when older students finger-point, it can indicate reading struggles and interfere with reading fluency (C). Having students turn bookmarks or popsicle sticks sideways to mark each line of text helps them transition past finger-pointing (D).

35. A: Experts recommend that instructional plans for teaching the alphabetic principle include practice opportunities for both new letter-sound relationships and cumulative reviews of relationships taught earlier; teaching letter-sound correspondences to children explicitly, and in isolation, before applying them to words (B); giving children opportunities to practice these correspondences during daily lessons (C); and giving them opportunities to apply their progressive learning of these correspondences to reading familiar, phonetically spelled words (D).

36. D: It is not necessary for students with retrieving or naming problems to master all consonant letter-sound associations or all short vowel letter-sound associations to begin decoding closed-syllable words with the consonant-vowel-consonant (CVC) pattern. It is also not necessary for them to master all consonants and one to two vowels. Once they have mastered one to two *short* vowel sound-letter associations, like [a] and [i], and several high-frequency consonant sound-letter associations, like [t], [b], [s], [f], and [m], teachers can start this decoding instruction, also gradually adding more letter-sound associations and reviewing often.

37. B: Introducing sound-spellings (A) is for teaching students which written letters correspond to which spoken sounds, which they must know *before* learning to decode words. Discriminating individual phonemes within words (C) is for teaching students phonological awareness, which they also must have *before* decoding new words. Reviewing sound-spellings to overlearn them (D) is for phonics maintenance rather than word decoding. Blending phonemes into words (B) is for helping students learn a strategy to apply their sound-spelling learning to decoding unfamiliar words.

38. C: Children often invent spellings during early learning. Though vowels are needed to decode words, these invented spellings frequently omit vowels (A); therefore, children need a great deal of practice to hear vowel sounds in words. Children can discriminate long vowel sounds more easily than short vowel sounds, not vice versa (B). Hence (though many phonics programs start with short vowels), phonological discrimination exercises should often focus on discriminating long vowels before short vowels, not vice versa (D).

39. A: Literacy research funded by the US Department of Education finds that systematic, explicit phonics instruction significantly improves children's reading comprehension, as well as both word recognition and spelling (B), and is especially effective for children having trouble learning to read (C). It does not, however, constitute a whole language reading program (D). Whole Language approaches focus on all aspects of language from a top-down approach, usually targeting whole words and application-based activities before targeting more minute skills, such as phonics. Explicit instruction in phonics is more of a bottom-up approach to language acquisition.

40. B: Closed syllables, i.e., those ending in a consonant and typically preceded by a short vowel sound (e.g., *fabric, rabbit*), are the syllable pattern type used most often, so they should be taught first, before open (A) or other syllable types. To teach from simpler to more complex, instruction in decoding multisyllabic words should also teach strategies for syllabication divisions after introducing multisyllabic words, not before (C). Also, teachers should teach spelling generalizations based on syllable pattern types, not vice versa (D).

41. D: Choice A indicates that the student is using semantic cues to construct meaning. Choice B indicates the student is using syntactic cues to construct meaning. Choice C indicates the student is using phonics cues to construct meaning. Choice D indicates the student is using (visual) graphophonic cues, i.e., whether word spellings match their phonetic sounds.

42. C: The general rule about splitting doubled consonants pertains most to syllabication, i.e., where to divide words up into their component syllables to inform pronunciation and meaning. Structural analysis (A) pertains to dividing words into component parts like prefixes, roots, and suffixes, which may or may not coincide with syllable divisions. Using common spelling patterns (B) pertains to determining meaning and pronunciation in unfamiliar words by comparing their spelling to the same or similar spellings in familiar words. Using morphemes (D) pertains to identifying the smallest meaningful grammatical units in words, e.g., *-ed* verb endings signify past tense.

43. D: The surrounding sentences will help the student determine word meaning; e.g., "The farmer will *sow* the vegetable seeds" vs. "She was like a *sow* nursing piglets." The sentence syntax and grammatical structure (B) will help by indicating parts of speech, which differ by meaning in this case. In the two example sentences given earlier, the first meaning is a verb, and the second is a noun. The verb has an auxiliary verb and direct object, and the noun has an article. Dictionary definitions (C) will help if the student does not already know one or both word meanings, or if the definition includes word-in-sentence examples resembling the text sentence(s).

44. B: What may seem contradictory actually just includes two aspects: on the one hand, denotative meaning is synonymous with dictionary definition (D); many sources define the former as the latter. On the other hand, dictionaries do not only provide denotative word meanings (A) or only connotative word meanings (C). Many dictionaries provide both denotative and connotative meanings for a word, with examples of each in sentences (B).

45. A: The more words a student can recognize automatically when reading, the more fluently he or she reads, with better comprehension; these in turn dramatically enhance the student's ability to recall the reading more accurately, with greater organization and detail. Fluency without understanding (B), understanding without fluency (C), and improved recall without or regardless of fluency (D) are hence incorrect.

46. D: Literal comprehension is what text states overtly, e.g., story characters, event sequences, stated facts, etc. Choices A and B are examples of literal comprehension responses. Inferential comprehension is deeper or implicit meaning not explicitly stated, which readers must infer by considering text and drawing conclusions, e.g., unstated main ideas, cause-and-effect relationships, generalizations, and predictions. Choice C is an example of an inferential comprehension response. Evaluative comprehension requires readers to form opinions after analyzing text information. Choice D is an example of an evaluative comprehension response.

47. C: Multiple researchers have found that effective programs that promote independent reading by students in school, libraries, and at home share the common elements of access to varied material to appeal to all preferences and age levels, active parental involvement in student reading, collaborations among other significant adults in students' lives, and partnerships among community institutions. It is not just one of these (A) that effective programs commonly share, nor only two (D); and significant adults' collaboration is not more important than active parental involvement (B).

48. B: Students reflect in reader response journals after independent, not sustained silent, reading (A). Teachers can use journals to monitor student reading, check comprehension, discuss texts, and suggest additional books (B). Not all students know how to respond to text by writing. Teachers should initially model the process, including prompts, and post lists of these, model methods for generating personal topics without prompts through the year, and give students lists of these for reference (C) to keep in their journals. Teachers should advise students to read about 80 percent of the time and write about 20 percent of the time (D).

49. C: Educational researchers (cf. Pardede, 2011) observe that novels can be too long for public school classes to read in limited time (A). Students typically require extensive instruction and time to understand figurative devices and other unfamiliar language in poems (B). Though students can be assigned to read drama, it is often impracticable for crowded classes with limited hours to act out a play (D). In contrast, short stories (C) can be read in one sitting and typically have one plot, fewer characters than novels, and brief, not detailed, setting descriptions, making it easier for students to follow a storyline.

50. B: Some educators (e.g., Rheinschild, "Pyramid Reading") order basic literary analysis skills in a hierarchy of progressive difficulty, which are illustrated in a pyramid (similar in conception to Maslow's hierarchy of needs pyramid, from basic to advanced). As they are progressive, teachers should teach one skill at a time until students master it before moving up to the next (A) rather than trying to cover them all together (B). Throughout the school year, teachers should frequently re-teach all the skills using materials of progressively greater complexity (C). Additionally, teachers should frequently evaluate students' skills throughout the year (D).

51. A: Among instructional strategies defined by a master teacher (Robb, 2002), asking students open-ended questions about the texts they read is the most useful for helping students to read critically. Teaching students how to skim text for headings, subheadings, boldface, illustrations, captions, sidebars, the index, and other text features that give signs (B) of pertinent material is most useful for helping students locate information. Guiding students to make connections between text and their own personal experiences (D), everyday life (C), world events, and other texts is most useful for helping students understand the relevance of learning materials.

52. B: In the hand outline instructional strategy (cf. Cox, 2009), the thumb (A) represents the topic sentence. This is logical as the hand has only one thumb, and it is a small but important part. The palm (C) represents the main idea, which is logical since it is a single, important, and larger part. The back of the hand (D) is not used, since a two-dimensional drawing would require drawing two hands or turning the paper over. The fingers (B) represent the supporting details, a logical match because there are multiple fingers on a hand and they are smaller than the palm.

53. B: The Directed Reading Thinking Activity, i.e., DRTA, is a comprehension strategy that helps students ask questions about text, make predictions about it, and then read to confirm or deny predictions. Gist (A) is a comprehension strategy that helps students identify the main idea, paraphrase, and summarize text. The Fishbowl (C) is an instructional strategy that helps students participate in classroom discussions. Cornell Notes (D) is an instructional strategy that helps students take notes, read text carefully, organize, and summarize information.

54. A: Descriptive writing, which is to "paint a picture" in words making something seem real to a reader's imagination, is more often included within narrative writing (A), i.e., storytelling like novels, short stories, biographies, etc. Other than certain character sketches, photo captions, ads, etc., most works are not entirely descriptive. Also, telling a story (like an anecdote) in the middle of descriptive writing could disrupt the description, since these have different purposes (B). Exposition is to inform or explain, so it typically does not include persuasive writing (C). Since narration's purpose is storytelling, it is less likely to include exposition (D).

55. C: When a student simply writes the parts of a composition in sequence (A), this is not recursive. Recursive writing repeats various parts of composition at any or all times during the process, including repeating some parts multiple times as needed. Thus brainstorming, outlining, writing, editing once, turning work in, and discarding it after it is graded (B) is not recursive. Always rigidly following the five stages (pre-writing, drafting, revising, editing, publishing) in sequence (D) precludes recursion. One example of recursive writing is when a student inserts another excellent point he or she suddenly thought of right before publishing (C).

56. D: Wallace et al. (*Reading Horizons,* V48.1, 2007) recommend four instructional strategies that use writing to improve student reading comprehension. About/point (C) is a summarizing strategy that helps students learn to differentiate main ideas from supporting details. Cubing (D) is a strategy that helps students learn to see information from various perspectives. Four square graphic organizer (B) is an organizational strategy that helps students make connections in content across the curriculum. Read, respond, revisit, discuss (A) is a strategy that helps students comprehend text by integrating reading, writing, and social interaction.

57. C: Stage 1, Emergent Spelling: 3 to 5-year-olds begin writing letters without phonemic matches; they learn drawing/writing differentiation, letter formation, writing directionality, and some letter-sound associations. Stage 2, Letter Name-Alphabetic Spelling: 5 to 7-year-olds learn the alphabetic principle, consonant and short vowel sounds, consonant blends, and digraphs. Stage 3, Within-Word Pattern Spelling: 7 to 9-year-olds learn long vowel spelling patterns, r-controlled vowels, more complex consonant patterns, diphthongs, and other less-frequent vowel patterns. Stage 4, Syllables and Affixes Spelling: 9 to 11-year-olds learn inflectional endings and rules, syllabication, and homophones. Stage 5, Derivational Relations Spelling: 11 to 14-year-olds learn consonant and vowel alternations, Greek and Latin roots and affixes, and etymologies.

58. A: The common spelling *-tion* reflects the frequently recurring pattern of reliable non-phonetic spelling patterns, because letters and phonemes do not match phonically. Recurring phonetic spelling patterns (B), contrastingly, are common spelling patterns with letters matching speech sounds. Etymological extensions to patterns (C) add to phonetic spelling patterns with spellings based on word origins. Spellings for Greek and Latin stems (D) help students learn how to spell many English words sharing common roots, whose spellings may be phonetic or non-phonetic (just as the Latin suffix *-tion* is non-phonetic).

59. D: Using quotation marks around quotations, and around certain types of titles, is an appropriate goal for students in grades 3-5. Using periods after declarative sentences (A), using question marks after interrogative sentences (B), and using commas to divide series of words (C) are all appropriate benchmarks for students in grades K-2.

60. B: Students gain deeper understanding and critical engagement by being exposed to various perspectives and learning to evaluate and compare sources relative to a topic. A is incorrect because it claims that direct learning about source types is the only benefit, which ignores the critical thinking benefits that students also gain. C is incorrect because the statement "how to build topic-related positions using evidence is not among benefits" is false; students do learn to construct evidence-based positions. D is incorrect because students gain insight into both selecting and evaluating sources, not just selection as implied by the option.

61. C: Teachers need to advise students that when they take research notes on information sources, they should note all details of the source material rather than taking more generalized notes (A), and differentiate clearly not only between quotations and paraphrases (B), but also between their own paraphrases and their own commentaries (D). Essentially, they must clearly differentiate among direct quotations from sources, their own paraphrases of statements in sources, and their own commentaries on those source statements (C).

62. A: By demonstrating or using think-alouds, the teacher should first model identifying and recording (e.g.) three research questions, then referring to the table of contents and headings in a text selected for this purpose, then reading chapters identified from the previous step for pertinent information, and then classifying or categorizing the information he or she has found according to which of the three questions it answers.

63. B: This trend has merit in the fact that it allows students to use the resources they already have instead of artificially suppressing the use of technology. Choice A is incorrect because, while not all students have phones, many do. Smartphones are among the most popular, ubiquitous, convenient, and mobile of devices that individuals use. Over time, smartphones have become increasingly prevalent, demonstrating that they are not considered too expensive in general. While it is unreasonable to expect all students to have their own phones, if device usage becomes fully integrated into curriculum, those who do not have access to a phone could be supplied by the school, in a similar fashion to classroom tablets or computers. Choice C is incorrect because device usage plays a big role in instruction, privacy, and safety for students. It is crucial to have acceptable use policies in place for technology. The scenario does not describe the school policy, but teachers who want to integrate technology into instruction must follow district and campus policies to ensure the legality of the practice and safety of the students. Choice D is incorrect as student privacy is inherently tied to the use of personal devices. A teacher should be able to give guidance to students on how to use any appropriate technology, and would ideally have a direct line of communication about classwork, but teachers should not expect to have complete access to students' personal devices.

64. B: Although concurrent learning disabilities and disorders are common, e.g., attentional, receptive, and expressive language difficulties often coexist, an expressive language disorder (A) would have the most direct impact on a student's speaking and writing performance and instruction. A receptive language disorder (B) would have the most direct impact on a student's listening and reading skills. An articulation disorder (C) would have the most direct impact on a student's correct or intelligible speech production or pronunciation. A movement disorder (D) could have impacts on speech production, but by itself it should not affect language or reading development.

65. A: Not all world cultures have spoken languages (B); e.g., deaf cultures sign but do not speak. Not all cultures have written languages (C); e.g., some island and tribal cultures have exclusively oral traditions, with no formal system of written symbols. All world cultures use social conventions and body language (D)—though the meanings of gestures vary across cultures more than facial expressions, all cultures use them—AND all cultures use some kind of language, whether it is spoken, written, signed (A), or any combination of these.

66. A: Recent research shows that dyslexia and similar reading disorders are primarily neurodevelopmental in origin, i.e., mainly due to neurological and developmental rather than environmental factors. Environmental deprivation of early exposure to reading activities can delay literacy development, but most (85 percent of) diagnosed learning problems are based in difficulties with reading and other language skills.

67. C: When a student has trouble recognizing words out of context (A), this is mainly a sign that the student has problems with decoding words, as is slow, laborious oral reading (B). Having trouble differentiating main ideas or important information from minor details (C) in text is mainly a sign that the student has problems with reading comprehension. Having trouble relating text to his or her own existing knowledge (D) often reflects difficulty using background knowledge, which can influence comprehension but is conceptually distinct from basic comprehension skills such as identifying main ideas.

68. D: When teaching sight words to students with moderate and severe intellectual disabilities, it has been found that community-based instruction helps promote generalization of skills. Generalization is when a student learns a skill in one context and begins to apply it to new contexts, incorporating it more generally into their thought processes. Students with intellectual disabilities may struggle more to apply skills to broader situations. For instance, they may be successful in learning sight words in the classroom, but they may leave that skill in the classroom instead of applying it out in the community. To help support the generalization process, this student's community should help reinforce that instruction out in the community to demonstrate that the skill can be used in all of life. Choices A and C are incorrect because they are not found to be as effective for students with disabilities as augmented practices, such as community-based instruction. Choice B is incorrect, as orthography refers to the actual writing of letters and less to do with reading skills, and especially sight words. Some teaching strategies may pair reading and writing skills together, but this is even less common for sight word instruction.

69. B: According to accepted educational measurement principles, teachers should design tests to measure ALL their learning objectives (including through a combination of tests), not just a few (A). While tests' primary uses are diagnosis or evaluation, another principle is that an important additional use is instructional (B), by enabling teachers to identify and re-teach important information students have missed, stimulate additional topic discussions, and integrate instruction and evaluation. Criterion-referenced tests measure achievement relative to preset criteria; norm-referenced tests enable group comparisons (C). Test validity and reliability are both equally necessary (D).

70. D: Testing instrument reliability is indicated if the test yields consistent results across repeated administrations. Measuring the specific skill that it claims to measure (A) indicates test validity, not reliability. Tests with clearly written items are typically more reliable than those using open-ended, ambiguous questions (B). Tests that measure a skill using a fairly large quantity of items are typically more reliable than tests using only a few, very focused items (C).

71. D: Researchers have found that explicit instruction in phonics does help students at risk for reading failure particularly, but also promotes higher achievement by all students (A). Research supports the use of decodable books (B) early in first grade. Studies find that the kind of text read by students affects the word identification strategies they use (C), and also that prior student literacy knowledge (indicated by reading readiness assessment), as well as using decodable texts early, contribute to developing understanding of sound-spelling relationships (D).

72. A: Researchers have found giving teachers practice (B) with skills under simulated conditions, both in workshop and controlled classroom settings, benefits teachers. However, even practice combined with structured feedback (D), another necessary component, would enable transfer of skills for fewer than 20 percent of participants. Modeling (C) and demonstrations of instructional procedures and lessons would enable transfer for 10 percent more participants. But without direct in-classroom coaching (A), NO teachers could transfer new skills to classrooms; hence this component is 100 percent necessary for transfer.

73. C: Experts advise that to differentiate reading instruction, teachers should not just reserve read-aloud materials for fun, but use them as common teaching texts (A) for building background knowledge, demonstrating strategy application, introducing issues, and inviting students to journal responses to issues, enabling all students to access needed reading skills and information. They should teach units using multiple texts to meet diverse reading levels (B); reserve 15-30 minutes at least three times a week for independent practice reading at student comfort levels (C); and organize units around topics, issues, or genres instead of basing them on the text (D).

74. B: Reading curriculum designs may fail when one or more of their individual components fail (A); or when their components do not fail individually, but are incompatible with one another (C); or when personnel charged with implementing a design dislike or misunderstand it (D). Since there are multiple sources of failure, most curriculum designs are neither 100 percent failures nor 100 percent successes—informing the fact that an essential element of designing curriculum is to provide for continuous improvement (B), during and following the design process.

75. D: To establish literacy-rich environments, experts advise teachers to label everything in the classroom with words and pictures. This helps students connect all things and places with written language representing them, rather than distracts (A). Directions, calendars, signs, and schedules are not only everyday organizational tools; teachers can also have students use them to understand everyday language use (B). Word and picture labels should not be avoided, but should include textured materials, Braille, large fonts, etc., enabling access for visually impaired students (C). If teachers and students redesign classrooms to reflect themes or books they have studied, students "live in" lessons, experiencing them directly (D).

76. C: Among main strategies for effective partnerships, the NEA identifies the following. First, schools collaborate with community members to establish consensus and develop action plans together, not on their own (A). Second, schools provide data-based, on-site professional development to promote collaboration of teachers with parents and other stakeholders, not just other teachers (B). Schools also study school and student data to examine current achievement trends and address student needs areas (C). Finally, schools strategically recruit community buy-in and partners from organizations, businesses, public officials, local leaders, religious organizations, social service agencies, and colleges to improve student learning, etc. (D).

77. A: From a literature review, researchers (c. Henderson and Mapp, 2002) concluded that students whose families are involved in their learning get higher grades, take more advanced classes, have higher graduation rates, and are more likely to attend postsecondary education. Students perform best academically when their parents adopt varied roles in their learning, like not only participating in school events and activities, but also helping at home, contributing to key school program decisions, guiding children through the system, etc. (B). Students with involved families also attend school more regularly, have more positive attitudes toward school, and demonstrate better behavior in school (C). Finally, students from diverse backgrounds perform better academically from school-family collaboration to bridge cultural gaps (D).

78. A: The NEA recommends that to promote family educational involvement at the school district level, meeting diverse family needs systemically includes providing interpreting and translating services. Supporting wrap-around community services is for meeting student health and social as well as academic needs (B). Supporting district-wide policies to promote effective partnerships among schools, families, and communities includes committing funding, professional development, and other resources (C) that enable functional implementation. District collaborative work on policies and practices should accord first priority to school sites with the highest needs (D).

79. C: To aid in consensus-building, a facilitator should always be neutral and, like a referee, should inform members of their adopted ground rules and intervene if somebody violates them. Although some skilled group members may fulfill this role, experts generally find this invites the possibility of non-neutrality and using the position unfairly to further one's own interests (D) at the expense of others' interests. The trend is increasingly toward hiring trained, skilled outsiders, but this is not always what occurs or is required (B).

80. C: Conflict is often viewed as negative, but this view is neither necessary nor accurate (A); conflict is natural in human interactions and can be viewed as an opportunity for social reform and moral growth (C). Conflict cannot be avoided (A), as it is ubiquitous in everyday life as well as educational decisions. Experts observe that understanding oneself is an essential basis for resolving conflict (B) through negotiation and cooperation. While conflict commonly occurs, it has been described more often than analyzed, not vice versa (D).

Constructed Response

1. Essay question graders commonly look for the following elements in a strong response: strong content knowledge, clear organization, and effective arguments or examples. Language and usage are not usually strictly graded, but they can make a big impact on the clarity of your ideas.

Please use the provided rubric to make sure your response meets these common criteria. Try to have a friend or family member grade your response for you or take a break after writing your response and return to grade it with fresh eyes.

Constructed Response Rubric

Domain	Description
Content Knowledge	• The response directly addresses every part of the prompt. • The response demonstrates independent knowledge of the topic. • The response discusses the topic at an appropriate depth.
Organization	• The response introduces the topic, usually with a thesis statement or by restating the prompt. • The response directly addresses the prompt by providing a clear and concise answer or solution. • The answer or solution is supported by logical arguments or evidence. • The response restates the main idea in the conclusion.
Arguments and Examples	• The response provides a reasonable answer to the prompt. • The answer is supported by strong reasoning or evidence. • The response develops ideas logically and connects ideas to one another. • The reasoning and evidence provided act to support a unified main idea.
Language and Usage	• The response demonstrates effective use of grammar and uses varied sentence structure throughout the response. • The response demonstrates correct use of spelling, punctuation, and capitalization. • The response demonstrates strong and varied use of vocabulary relevant to the topic and appropriate for the intended audience.

2. Essay question graders commonly look for the following elements in a strong response: strong content knowledge, clear organization, and effective arguments or examples. Language and usage are not usually strictly graded, but they can make a big impact on the clarity of your ideas.

Please use the provided rubric to make sure your response meets these common criteria. Try to have a friend or family member grade your response for you or take a break after writing your response and return to grade it with fresh eyes.

Constructed Response Rubric

Domain	Description
Content Knowledge	• The response directly addresses every part of the prompt. • The response demonstrates independent knowledge of the topic. • The response discusses the topic at an appropriate depth.
Organization	• The response introduces the topic, usually with a thesis statement or by restating the prompt. • The response directly addresses the prompt by providing a clear and concise answer or solution. • The answer or solution is supported by logical arguments or evidence. • The response restates the main idea in the conclusion.
Arguments and Examples	• The response provides a reasonable answer to the prompt. • The answer is supported by strong reasoning or evidence. • The response develops ideas logically and connects ideas to one another. • The reasoning and evidence provided act to support a unified main idea.
Language and Usage	• The response demonstrates effective use of grammar and uses varied sentence structure throughout the response. • The response demonstrates correct use of spelling, punctuation, and capitalization. • The response demonstrates strong and varied use of vocabulary relevant to the topic and appropriate for the intended audience.

Practice Test #2

Multiple Choice Questions

1. Which of the following is important when using performance-based assessments of student literacy?

a. Establishing valid norms for student scoring
b. Establishing clear, equitable scoring criteria
c. Establishing single correct answers for items
d. Establishing standard answer keys for scores

2. In a rubric for scoring oral English language proficiency in English language learners (ELLs), which of these would most reflect a criterion at the highest proficiency level?

a. Being able to repeat English words and phrases
b. Being able to name concrete objects upon sight
c. Being able to participate in classroom discussions
d. Being able to communicate well in social contexts

3. Of the following, what is true about enabling students to participate actively in portfolio assessments?

a. Teachers can have students select their own work samples to reflect on their progress.
b. Teachers can give students performance criteria, but not let them help develop goals.
c. Teachers can have students create their own rubrics, but only in small or class groups.
d. Teachers can have students set realistic improvement goals but should not help them.

4. When assessing pre-reading skills in typically-developing preschoolers, which of the following skills should NOT be expected?

a. They should be able to recite the full alphabet.
b. They should be able to recite all numbers from 1-10.
c. They should be able to sound out three-lettered words.
d. They should be able to tell whether or not two words rhyme.

5. During informal assessment, which of these is the best example of print awareness in a young child?

a. The child can identify the front and the back of a book.
b. The child can identify all letters in the words in a book.
c. The child can identify words but not spaces in between.
d. The child can identify and read sentences with fluency.

6. A teacher conducts an informal one-to-one reading assessment of rhyme recognition with a young child. Which of the following should the teacher always do first?

a. Ask the child whether he or she knows what rhyming words are.
b. Ask the child to demonstrate by saying two rhyming words.
c. Give the child an explanation by defining what rhymes are.
d. Give the child an example of a pair of words that rhyme.

7. As an assessment, a teacher gives a student a cloze procedure. Which response is an example of a student reading strategy based primarily on using syntactic cues to meaning?

a. The missing word must be "telescope" because it ends with the root "scope" and the context has to do with things that are far away.
b. The missing word must be a bad thing, because the word describing it is "horrible."
c. The missing word must be an adjective because it is before the word that is a noun.
d. The missing word must be impossible to guess, because I read one word at a time.

8. When assessing oral reading fluency, which characteristic indicates a non-fluent reader?

a. Simultaneous word identification and comprehension
b. Automaticity and speed irrespective of expressiveness
c. Perceiving chunks of information, not individual words
d. Demonstrating an absence of effort with reading aloud

9. Which of the following aspects of reading comprehension belongs in the semantic language domain?

a. Grammar
b. Word order
c. Word meaning
d. Sentence structure

10. When planning instruction in reading and writing, what is most important?

a. Assignments that are tailored to individual student ability
b. Assignments that provide students with sufficient variety
c. Assignments that are uniform across students for fairness
d. Assignments that offer equal variety and individualization

11. Based on assessment findings, a teacher introduces her students to graphic organizers to help them understand concepts. Which of the following is NOT a way graphic organizers help students?

a. They present concepts in visual form.
b. They convert the verbal to numerical.
c. They help students compare, contrast, separate, and group concepts.
d. They enable students to classify or categorize concepts.

12. To promote phonics understanding and word-decoding skills, which teacher practice is most beneficial to younger, beginning, and struggling students?

a. Supply concrete objects or pictures and have them sort these phonemically.
b. Say aloud any phonemes whenever students identify or discriminate these.
c. Point out the letters and words in environmental printed or written materials.
d. Encourage them to guess unfamiliar words in print by their first one or two letters.

13. Which of the following is NOT a component of the reading workshop as a differentiated instruction approach?

a. The teacher models a specific cognitive skill or reading strategy.
b. The students apply a skill or strategy in reading assigned books.
c. The teacher conducts one-to-one conferences with students.
d. The students are afforded time to read books independently.

14. In the response to intervention (RTI) framework, which recommendations from the federal What Works Clearinghouse (WWC) apply to all three RTI tiers regarding primary-grades classroom reading instruction?

a. Intensive instruction
b. Small-group instruction
c. Differentiated instruction
d. Evidence-based instruction

15. Which of the following most accurately reflects the typical structure of a guided reading lesson as an alternative structure for differentiating reading instruction?

a. The text to read is selected by the students.
b. Students start reading without introduction.
c. Reading is guided, but there is no discussion.
d. Instruction for strategic activities is included.

16. Of the following, what is most characteristic of a skills-focused lesson structure as an alternative to differentiating reading instruction?

a. The lessons move at a slower pace.
b. The lessons are teacher-centered.
c. The lessons vary in skills by group.
d. The lessons only use small groups.

17. In the gradual release model of individual and group reading lessons, which represents the correct sequence of activities?

a. Modeling and demonstration, teacher-led collaboration, guided practice, student-led collaboration, independent practice
b. Guided practice, independent practice, teacher-led collaboration, student-led collaboration, modeling and demonstration
c. Teacher-led collaboration, student-led collaboration, modeling and demonstration, guided practice, independent practice
d. Independent practice, guided practice, student-led collaboration, teacher-led collaboration, modeling and demonstration

18. Four central components of reading instruction reflect various learning opportunities in comprehensive literacy programs. According to the LEAD21 program, what are these components?

a. Whole-class reading, small-group reading, paired reading, and individual reading done by the students
b. Reading to students, large student group reading, small student group reading, and independent reading by the student
c. Interactive and community reading or read-alouds, differentiated reading, guided reading, and independent reading
d. Heterogeneous group reading, homogeneous group reading, reading partnerships, individual reading

19. Among guiding principles of LEAD21's small-group reading instruction (SGRI), which is most accurately represented here?

a. The need for greater uniformity in reading instruction
b. The need for focus on progress more than proficiency
c. The need to inform instruction by periodic assessment
d. The need to accelerate progress to close learning gaps

20. The small-group reading instruction (SGRI) method used in LEAD21 classifies students into four reading levels for small groups relative to grade level. Which choice correctly shows their sequence from the lowest to highest reading level?

a. Intensive, strategic, benchmark, advanced
b. Strategic, intensive, advanced, benchmark
c. Benchmark, advanced, strategic, intensive
d. Advanced, intensive, benchmark, strategic

21. Which choice is correct regarding flexible grouping for reading instruction within and across classrooms?

a. Flexible grouping within the classroom is a homogeneous format.
b. Flexible grouping across classrooms has a heterogeneous format.
c. Flexible grouping within the classroom prohibits added resources.
d. Flexible grouping across classrooms can vary teachers for reading.

22. Regarding instruction in speaking and listening, which of these have researchers found about the relationship between the time people spend using these skills and the time schools spend developing them?

a. Schools spend more time developing these skills than people spend using them.
b. Schools spend about the same amount of time on these skills as people use them.
c. Schools spend an opposite amount of time that people use these skills on developing them.
d. Schools spend only slightly less time on teaching these skills than people spend to use them.

23. What are some things that teachers can have younger students do to develop, practice, and demonstrate skills for listening and speaking?

a. Have them retell stories that were read aloud.
b. Have them tell stories they have heard instead of making up stories.
c. Have them discuss story characters rather than pretend to be them.
d. Have them write their thoughts to show thought habits about content areas.

24. To raise student awareness of the nonverbal aspects of communication, of what can teachers correctly inform students?

a. 50 percent of our communication is verbal, and 50 percent is nonverbal.
b. 10 percent of our communication is verbal, and 90 percent is nonverbal.
c. 60 percent of our communication is verbal, and 40 percent is nonverbal.
d. 25 percent of our communication is verbal, and 75 percent is nonverbal.

25. Regarding speech pre-production learning activities that teachers can use with ELL students to encourage them to speak English, which of the following is accurate?

a. Choral readings afford advantages for beginning ELLs.
b. Echo reading is not spontaneous and thus not useful.
c. Shared reading and writing will not promote speech.
d. Singing is vocal but otherwise irrelevant to speaking.

26. According to typical state and district English language proficiency (ELP) standards in comprehending oral communications, active listening for learning by third-grade ELL students includes understanding and following directions related to physical movement in space. These differ by level in which respect(s)?

a. The number of steps a student can follow increases by level.
b. The number of dimensions of movement increases by level.
c. The numbers of both of these increase with ascending level.
d. The numbers of neither of these increase according to level.

27. Which of the following lists of symptoms is characteristic of a language disorder?

a. Omissions, additions, substitutions, or distortions of phonemes
b. Blocks, repetitions, or prolongations of sounds, words, and phrases
c. Difficulties with the loudness, pitch, or tone quality of the voice
d. Limited vocabulary, incorrect grammar, wrong word meanings

28. For an instructional activity to develop phonological awareness in K-1 students, which of these would teach them segmentation on multiple phonological levels?

a. Teaching children how to separate sentences into the individual words that make up each sentence
b. Teaching children to divide sentences into words, words into syllables, and syllables into phonemes
c. Teaching children to divide words into individual syllables, or to divide words into onsets and rimes
d. Teaching children how to separate short, monosyllabic words into individual component phonemes

29. Researchers have found which of these about instruction in phonological awareness?

a. All children benefit highly from receiving instruction in phonological awareness.
b. Children at risk for speech or language delays benefit the most from this teaching.
c. Some children benefit little from this instruction, and some do not benefit at all.
d. This instruction only benefits children who have normal language development.

30. According to experts, which of the following is an accurate distinction regarding phonological awareness and phonemic awareness?

a. Phonological awareness distinguishes speech sounds from meanings.
b. There is no real distinction; they are synonyms used interchangeably.
c. Phonological awareness involves sounds, phonemic involves speech.
d. Phonemic awareness is the less sophisticated level between the two.

31. Which of these statements is most applicable to instruction in phonemic awareness?

a. Instruction in phonemic awareness should be standardized across students since it is a basic skill.
b. Instruction in phonemic awareness should be uniform since children start school at similar levels.
c. Instruction in phonemic awareness should be individualized to address each child's specific needs.
d. Instruction in phonemic awareness should be less critical as it is unrelated to later reading ability.

32. What is the best way to utilize picture flashcards to develop children's phonemic awareness?

a. The flashcards that are used should have pictures unfamiliar to the child.
b. The child should be asked to identify a word's first and second phoneme.
c. The child should be asked only to identify the word name of each picture.
d. The flashcards should only be used for children with strong phonics skills.

33. Research shows that developmentally, which of these options is easiest for young children to identify?

a. The medial and final phonemes of words
b. The initial and medial phonemes of words
c. Only the medial phonemes of words
d. The initial and final phonemes of words

34. Which of these is true about using music to teach sight words to kindergarten students?

a. Singing words to catchy tunes is a mnemonic device.
b. Singing is fun for children but does not aid memory.
c. Singing helps retain new words but not the spellings.
d. Singing is an activity that young children do not like.

35. Which of the following is incorrect about teaching students the distinction between vowels as open sounds and consonants as closed sounds?

a. This should be taught for the first time when teaching letter-sound matching.
b. This should be introduced when initially teaching phonemic awareness.
c. This should be reviewed after teaching some letter shapes and names.
d. This should be reviewed after teaching some letter decoding.

36. Regarding instruction in letter-sound associations for students having difficulty with naming or recall, which is a recommended instructional strategy?

a. They should progress to new material quickly to maintain learning momentum.
b. These students will forget associations without extensive practice.
c. Students will become bored and lose motivation with overlearning.
d. Every lesson should focus on new material instead of on reviewing.

37. Which type of blending of phonemes into words is the best technique for diagnostically pinpointing individual student problem areas in phonics instruction?

a. Successive blending
b. Silent blending
c. Final blending
d. Line blending

38. In an oddity task to demonstrate student ability to identify words with the same and different initial, medial, and final phonemes in words, which of these asks students to identify words with the same medial consonant sound?

a. Identifying *pan* and *cat* from among *pan, top,* and *cat*
b. Identifying *lesson* and *missing* in *lesson, kitten, missing*
c. Identifying *feet* as different among *late, feet,* and *take*
d. Identifying *ten* and *man* from among *ten, sat,* and *man*

39. Government-funded research has found which of the following about phonics instruction?

a. It is equally effective regardless of whether it is systematic and explicit or not.
b. It is more effective for children of certain socioeconomic levels than for others.
c. It is equally effective regardless of the age or grade levels when introduced.
d. It is more effective when students can understand and apply their learning.

40. Which of the following words contains consonant digraphs but no consonant blends?

a. Shocking
b. Screams
c. Splashes
d. Smoking

41. A student is stumped by an unfamiliar word. The teacher guides the student to look for parts of the word that seem familiar. The student discovers a prefix, root, and suffix, each resembling those in other words she knows. Which instructional approach does this reflect?

a. Synthetic phonics
b. Onsets and rimes
c. Structural analysis
d. Analytic phonics

42. In an unfamiliar word encountered while reading, a student does not recognize the first part of the word, but does recognize that it ends in *-tion,* meaning it is a noun and the first part probably derives from a verb. Which term best describes the syllable *-tion*?

a. A phoneme
b. A morpheme
c. A grapheme
d. A sememe

43. Among these effective instructional strategies for building and extending vocabulary knowledge, which one is implicit?

a. Context skills
b. Root analysis
c. Word maps
d. Keywords

44. Students receive a new text full of technical terminology unfamiliar to them. Which reference source is likely to be most efficient in helping them understand these terms?

a. Encyclopedia
b. Dictionary
c. Thesaurus
d. Glossary

45. Of the following influences on student reading comprehension, which one is a psychological factor?

a. Attention
b. Perception
c. Motivation
d. Working memory

46. When can making a KWL chart help students with reading comprehension?

a. Before, during, and after students read
b. Before and during but not after reading
c. During and after but not before reading
d. Before and after but not during reading

47. National research data show which of these about the relationship of high school reading and academic achievement to parental involvement?

a. Students resent parents' checking their homework as an invasion of privacy.
b. Students often get higher English grades when parents discuss school plans.
c. Students rebel in adolescence against high parent educational expectations.
d. Students find discussing future plans with parents to cause undue pressure.

48. Explicit instruction in reading comprehension strategies is found more effective in research. Which component of explicit instruction is reflected when a teacher reads text the students are reading while conducting a "think-aloud?"

a. Modeling
b. Application
c. Guided practice
d. Direct explanation

49. Which of these accurately reflects research findings related to literary genre studies?

a. Research finds experience reading various genres unrelated to writing in various genres.
b. Research finds literary analysis requires applying different strategies and skills by genre.
c. Research finds analyzing different literary genres contributes to cognitive development.
d. Research finds deeper immersion in one to two genres more important than exposure to many.

50. Among reading materials teachers can select to promote student comprehension of nonfiction, most content-area textbooks used in public schools feature which type of writing?

a. Narrative
b. Persuasive
c. Descriptive
d. Informational

51. One instructional strategy to help students understand nonfiction is to teach them the elements of text structure and how to identify these by "signal" words. Among common text structures, which of these signal words indicate a descriptive structure?

a. Before, initially, secondly, next, then, last, after, finally
b. For example, in particular, specifically, and in addition
c. In comparison to, similar to, likewise, however
d. Therefore, consequently, why, because, may be due to

52. Students read a text wherein the author presents a point; provides evidence to support it; appeals to reader emotion, logic, or belief in author credibility; and raises and refutes a counterpoint. Based on this description, the students can identify author purpose as which of these?

a. To inform the audience
b. To entertain the reader
c. To persuade the reader
d. To analyze the subject

53. To help students find and use evidence from nonfictional text to support their ideas, which instructional strategy is most applicable?

a. Inquiry Charts (I-Charts)
b. Graphic organizers
c. Journaling
d. RAFT

54. In writing instruction, which of these correctly represents some of the things that teachers should instruct students to consider about the audience for whom they will be writing?

a. They must consider who will read it, but the format (oral presentation, blog, school newspaper, etc.) is irrelevant.
b. They must consider reading level(s), vocabulary, and writing length the audience expects more than the message.
c. They must consider the message they want to convey more than the format in which the audience will receive it.
d. They must consider the type of writing that their intended audience will expect as much as who that audience is.

55. Which of the following is true about giving students effective feedback during all stages of the writing process?

a. Students are more receptive to feedback from their parents than feedback from their teachers.
b. Students explore all possibilities in their compositions when teachers treat writing as a process.
c. Students will not realize any greater benefits from feedback if teachers divide writing into steps.
d. Students are able to maintain more perspective about their work by viewing writing as a whole.

56. Among principles of effective writing instruction, which of these reflects teaching discourse knowledge that enables more effective student writing?

a. Varying levels of explicit instruction, using small groups, and varying amounts of writing instruction time
b. Allowing sufficient time for systematic writing opportunities in both ELA classes and all content subjects
c. Incorporating reasons and methods for explicit writing instruction, including feedback and collaboration
d. Organizing writing effectively for various subjects, plus spelling, vocabulary, syntax, etc., for the subjects

57. In which stage of spelling development do children typically learn the alphabetic principle?

a. In Stage 1
b. In Stage 3
c. In Stage 2
d. In Stage 4

58. A student can determine how to spell words like *psychology, psychiatrist, psychotic, psychopath, psychoactive,* etc., because they all start with the same Greek-derived prefix. This illustrates which type of spelling strategy?

a. Morphemic spelling strategies
b. Rule-based spelling strategies
c. Phonetic spelling strategies
d. Visual spelling strategies

59. In which of the following mechanical writing conventions should teachers instruct typically developing students in grades K-2?

a. Capitalizing salutations and closings in letters
b. Capitalizing the initial word of each sentence
c. Capitalizing names of months and weekdays
d. Capitalizing names of holidays and countries

60. Which of these is most accurate about the research skill of formulating a research question?

a. Students typically have no problem translating their source readings into writing.
b. Teachers should begin by having students form questions on discussed concepts.
c. Teachers should begin by having students form questions from assignment topics.
d. Students may find certain graphic organizers helpful for this, but not mind-maps.

61. What is a valid guideline for teachers to follow in instructional activities that help students practice evaluating information sources?

a. Practicing evaluation during ongoing discussion can engage students more deeply.
b. Practicing evaluation should be reserved until after students have discussed topics.
c. Teachers should provide long, complete passages from different topical resources.
d. Students should evaluate material using unlimited numbers of open-ended questions.

62. A fourth-grade teacher instructs students in how to locate and use information sources to answer their research questions. In this process, which of the following relates to the step of guided practice?

a. The teacher has students write research questions, find sources, take notes, and make outlines.
b. The teacher has students make outlines from their notes and classify information with support.
c. The teacher asks students how they located information and they respond, describing all steps.
d. The teacher demonstrates identifying questions, finding information, and how to categorize it.

63. A teacher who has integrated student smartphone use into the curriculum for doing research and completing assignments recommends a virtual field trip as an introductory activity for educators wanting to follow suit. What can teachers and students do during this activity?

a. Teachers can have students find more information by visiting a website, not a computer lab.
b. Teachers can locate experts in pertinent fields, but they will not speak directly with students.
c. Teachers can record the calls, but students cannot hear both ends of a teacher conversation.
d. Teachers can have students ask their own questions to direct the ending of the conversation.

64. What has research found about appropriately challenging, effective instruction for high achievers?

a. Low-income high achievers are less likely to attend college.
b. High achievers should be given highly directive assignments.
c. Students may collaborate across classes or even grade levels.
d. Differentiation requires more supports for the higher grades.

65. According to principles of educational measurement as applied to reading assessment, what is the most logical sequence for the following practices?

a. Develop assessments, design curricula, adopt standards, set goals
b. Set goals, adopt standards, design curricula, develop assessments
c. Adopt standards, set goals, develop assessments, design curricula
d. Design curricula, adopt standards, set goals, develop assessments

66. Among specific components of reading difficulties, which category is a result of the other two?

a. Difficulties with decoding words
b. Difficulties with comprehending
c. Difficulties with retention of text
d. Difficulties with all are unrelated

67. Which of these is one of the signs that a student has difficulty with retaining reading?

a. The student's oral reading disregards punctuation.
b. The student's reading omits, or disregards, details.
c. The student's insertion of additional words that are not in the text is frequent.
d. The student's connection of text ideas is deficient.

68. What have research studies found about computer-assisted instruction (CAI) programs for teaching reading and communication skills to students with various disabilities?

a. These programs increase reading skills but decrease interaction.
b. Multimedia software plus scaffolding teach this population less.
c. CAI with the Nonverbal Reading Approach was the most useful.
d. Student differences make individualizing instruction paramount.

69. Which of the following is a way of determining that a reading assessment instrument is valid?

a. The test items minimize guesswork by students.
b. The test items measure the indicated construct.
c. The test items are sufficiently large in numbers.
d. The test items give consistent scores over time.

70. Researchers have identified which of the following about norm-referenced reading tests?

a. They are better for assessing abstract cognitive levels.
b. They are better for assessing in homogeneous groups.
c. They are better for assessing narrow ranges of ability.
d. They are better for assessing limited outcome ranges.

71. Regarding effective reading programs, which of these is most accurate?

a. Among programs claiming that they are based on research, the majority actually are.
b. Among programs claiming that they balance literature and phonics, most of them do.
c. Among programs claiming instructional integrity, teachers can believe all such claims.
d. Among programs claiming balance, teachers need research-based evaluation criteria.

72. In implementing a new school reading program, school leaders and leadership teams must rise to the challenge of managing teacher "domestication" of the new program—i.e., altering its design to do it their own way, which frequently decreases its effectiveness—when during its implementation?

a. During the third year of its implementation
b. During the first year of its implementation
c. During the second year of implementation
d. During the fourth year of implementation

73. To differentiate reading instruction, which of the following do educational experts recommend?

a. Concentrating on having students memorize facts rather than spend time discussing reading
b. Assigning all students to write following lessons or demonstrations to inform intervention plans
c. Modeling how to construct meaning from text during read-alouds, one on one, and with small groups
d. First collecting student reading matter and read-aloud texts, and then planning units of study

74. Which of these best describes characteristics of K-12 curriculum designs for reading?

a. Designing a K-12 reading curriculum requires following a series of steps in rigid order.
b. Regardless of systematic planning and inventive thinking, compromises are inevitable.
c. Curriculum design decisions made at separate stages are independent of one another.
d. Conceptualizing curriculum design precedes specifications, development, and refinement.

75. What description best represents how teachers promote language, literacy, and reading development by integrating it into their classroom instruction?

a. The teacher asks students during a science lesson to state hypotheses, observations, and conclusions orally.
b. The teacher asks students during a science lesson to write down hypotheses, observations, and conclusions.
c. The teacher models language and literacy participation by demonstrating writing apart from class discussion.
d. The teacher provides games that require students read, write, and act out target content in small groups.

76. The National Education Association (NEA) identifies a number of strategies for schools to form effective family and community partnerships. For example, one is to use culturally appropriate outreach targeting the concerns of high-needs students, schools, and communities. What is another strategy?

a. Schools take time to build one-to-one family-educator relationships, discuss, and agree to optimal collaboration for students.
b. Schools take care not to set or communicate high or rigorous expectations that intimidate at-risk or marginal students.
c. Schools require teachers and educational support professionals to overcome barriers of culture, class, and language.
d. Schools establish community connections to offer students relevant, hands-on learning, not for community service.

77. A review of the research literature has found which of the following about the influence of continuing family involvement in education on students in grades 6-12?

a. Middle school and high school students with involved families adjust to new schools like others.
b. Middle school and high school students with involved families always increase the work quality.
c. Middle school and high school students with involved families make more realistic future plans.
d. Middle school and high school students with involved families have equal odds of dropping out.

78. Which of these does the NEA recommend to promote research-based strategies for developing school partnerships with families and communities at the national level?

a. Policy forums and conferences should include provisions for partnerships, but legislative and policy proposals should not.
b. Educators and families must advocate with federal legislators for partnerships, but these do not belong in federal law.
c. Members of the NEA should disseminate recommended partnership strategies to non-members, not fellow members.
d. School reform initiatives should center around the subject of partnerships among schools, families, and communities.

79. Mr. Rivera has just received a new student that has been identified as an intermediate-level ELL. Which of the following does he have the legal and professional responsibility to provide this student?

a. Linguistic support services to provide equal access to learning opportunities
b. Language objectives and a detailed plan to achieve them
c. Access to a qualified interpreter to translate instruction
d. The opportunity to take assessments in his or her primary language

80. When educators and other stakeholders disagree about a school reading program, conflict resolution may be necessary or helpful. Which is the LEAST productive way of responding to conflict?

a. Team building
b. Principled negotiation
c. Positional negotiation
d. Conflict transformation

Constructed Response

1. Scenario: You are the reading specialist at a public high school. Recent school data have identified a disproportionate number of students scoring significantly below their grade levels in reading. The principal asks you to organize and supervise a new school-wide reading program.

- Describe one strategy apiece for how you will (1) plan, (2) organize, (3) coordinate, and (4) supervise the reading program on a school-wide level. Explain the rationale for each strategy.

- Describe one example each of (1) a principle, (2) a procedure, and (3) an issue related to the design, implementation, or evaluation of the new reading program. Summarize the reason for the principle, the purpose of the procedure, and one suggested response to the issue.

2. Scenario: You are a reading specialist in an elementary school. Lacey is a first-grade student whose teacher asks you to evaluate her current literacy development. The teacher would also appreciate your suggesting some instructional strategies she could use to enhance her literacy progress.

Lacey has already learned more sight words than most of her classmates. When she does not recognize a word by sight, she most often uses book illustrations, pictures, and other visual information to help her understand text. When the teacher reads aloud to the class, however, Lacey appears confused and cannot answer questions about the text immediately following the read-aloud. The teacher reports a large disparity between Lacey's excellent ability to recognize words by sight—and figure out new word and simple sentence meanings using visual clues—and her difficulties with understanding the words and sentences that she hears.

Using the information from this scenario and the documents below, write a response analyzing this case study and addressing these two tasks:

a. Identify and describe one strength in literacy and one need in literacy for Lacey. Support these by citing evidence from the scenario and documents provided. Note: The disorder the teacher suspects in her last anecdotal note is correct. When describing Lacey's need, include an explanation of this disorder's impact on her listening skills.

b. Identify and describe one instructional strategy to offer the teacher that will address the literacy need you identified in the previous task, while also making use of the literacy strength you identified, to further Lacey's literacy development.

DOCUMENT 1:

Reading Passage and Questions for Informal Assessment

This passage is from a first-grade Life Science textbook with a Lexile Level number appropriate for students reading at grade level. Lacey has neither heard nor seen it before. First you ask Lacey to listen while you read it aloud. When you ask her the accompanying questions orally, she misses three of four. Then, you ask Lacey to read the passage silently herself and answer the accompanying questions by reading them on paper or screen and circling or clicking the correct answers. This time, she gets all four questions correct.

Baby Elephant Behaviors

Elephants live all across Africa and parts of Asia. Baby elephants are called calves (or a calf). Elephant calves are not able to fend for themselves, so they rely on their parents to protect them and find food.

Calves are very curious. They like to mimic older elephants to learn how to behave. They like to play, run, and carry around toys. Sometimes, curious calves will even take food out of other elephants' mouths to taste a new food!

Calves drink milk and stay by their mothers' sides until they are at least two years old. As they grow up, they keep close to their relatives until they are finally big and strong enough to go out on their own.

Questions:

1. What is a calf?

a) A baby elephant
b) A teenage elephant
c) A grown-up elephant

2. The passage describes a young elephant's behavior. Which of the following seems like a young elephant's behavior?

a) It likes to play and roll in the mud.
b) Its eyes are closed and it does not have much hair.
c) It can swim and find its own food.

3. If a calf still drinks milk, what do we know about it?

a) The calf was born this year.
b) The calf is younger under three years old.
c) The calf cannot eat fruit yet.

4. What is "Baby Elephant Behaviors" mostly about?

a) What baby elephant personalities and behaviors are like
b) What a newborn elephant likes to eat
c) What the life of an elephant looks like

DOCUMENT 2:

Teacher's anecdotal notes

September: Lacey loves picture books. She can tell stories based on the pictures. She can also read simple text in storybooks with pictures at the early first-grade level. She identifies words easily on sight.

October: Over the past month, I have observed a pattern whenever I read aloud to the class: Lacey seems to have great difficulty understanding what she hears. She is not inattentive or distracted; she appears to concentrate very hard. She gets more meaning from looking at words than from listening to them. She uses pictures to get added information about text, but she also recognizes many words on sight. She does not recognize these same words when hearing them read or spoken aloud.

November: I have been trying to use visual modalities with Lacey to supplement her reading and writing instruction, but I am at a bit of a loss as to how to help her with listening skills. One of the specialists mentioned central auditory processing disorder, and I am wondering if this is what Lacey has. I need evaluations by the reading specialist and SLP to assess needs and recommend instructional supports. We may also want to refer the student to a specialist for a diagnosis.

Answer Key and Explanations for Test #2

Multiple Choice Questions

1. B: Performance-based assessments do not involve comparing student performance to norms (A) as standardized tests do. Rather, they evaluate each student's (in this case, literacy) skills based on how that student performs or by products he or she produces. Thus, teachers must establish clear, equitable criteria (B) for evaluating these, because there will not be a single correct answer (C). Student responses will vary widely, so teachers must use these criteria plus their own judgment, not standardized answer keys (D).

2. C: Being able to repeat English words and phrases (A) and name concrete objects on sight (B) are both examples of criteria at the lowest level of an oral ELP scoring rubric. Being able to communicate well in social contexts (D) is an example of a rubric criterion for an intermediate ELP level. At the highest level, the student would communicate *very* well, not only in social but also academic contexts. Being able to participate in classroom discussions (C) is an example of the highest ELP level.

3. A: One way teachers can enable active student participation in portfolio assessments is to have students select samples from their own work to reflect on their development over time. Another is to give students criteria for performance to aim for and let them collaborate with teachers to develop goals (B) and standards for themselves. Another is to have students create their own rubrics—in small groups, as a whole class, or individually (C). Setting realistic, tangible goals for improvement, collaboratively with teachers (D), is another way of engaging active student participation.

4. C: When assessing pre-reading skills in typically developing preschoolers, they should be able to demonstrate some benchmarks. Though they are somewhat flexible, most pre-schoolers are able to demonstrate knowledge of the full-alphabet, often in song-form. They are usually able to count from 1 to 10. They are often able to recognize some sight words, though these are not usually tied to phonetic skills at this age. Preschoolers may recognize some words as whole units, but it is unlikely that they will be able to sound out words from their letter components. Preschoolers do usually have a good grasp of similar sounds and can usually distinguish between rhyming word pairs and non-rhyming word pairs.

5. A: One good indication of print awareness in a young child during informal assessment is that the child can identify the front and back of a book. Another is that the child can identify one letter in a word in the book, not all letters in words (B). Another is that the child can identify both words in a book, and the spaces between them (C). Print awareness in a young child does not mean the child can read sentences fluently (D), or even words yet: awareness of print concepts is a prerequisite for learning to read.

6. A: The *first* thing the teacher should do is always to ask the child if he or she knows what rhyming words are. If the child answers yes, the teacher should ask the child to say two rhyming words (B). If the child gives an incorrect example, or has answered no to the question, the teacher should then explain to the child the definition of rhymes (C). After explaining, the teacher should then give the child an example of two rhyming words (D). The teacher can then offer other word pairs and have the child identify whether they rhyme or not. Once the child masters this, the teacher can ask the child to say two rhyming words again.

7. C: Choice A is an example of a student reading strategy based on morphology and semantic clues to determine the appropriate prefix. Choice B is an example of using semantic cues to meaning: "horrible" more likely modifies "disaster," "mess," "mistake," etc., than "happiness," "celebration," "opportunity," etc. Choice C is an example of using syntactic cues to meaning: in English, standard word order dictates that adjectives precede nouns. Choice D is an example of decoding difficulties or reading only one word at a time, which interfere with student reading strategies using grammatical, syntactic, or semantic cues to meaning.

8. B: Fluent readers are able to recognize and understand words at the same time (A). While they recognize words more automatically and quickly, they also comprehend overall meaning, enabling them to use natural, conversational expression accordingly. Hence, students who read aloud in expressionless monotones, despite speed and automaticity, do not read fluently (B). This is typically because they must decode individual words, whereas fluent readers organize words into chunks of meaningful information (C). Whereas non-fluent readers read laboriously, fluent readers read effortlessly (D).

9. C: Semantics primarily refers to word meaning, often with a focus on the individual word, but sometimes including sentence and paragraph context. Any aspect of language that is used to convey meaning can technically considered a semantic property of language. Grammar, word order, and sentence structure are all aspects of syntax.

10. D: When planning reading and writing instruction, it is equally important to tailor assignments to the abilities of each individual student (A) and to vary assignments enough (B) to keep students engaged; address different learning styles, interests, and preferences; and expose students to different literacy experiences. Assignment uniformity across students does not ensure but prevents fairness (C), as student strengths and needs differ individually.

11. B: Graphic organizers help students understand concepts by presenting abstract ideas in visual form (A), making them easier to comprehend through pictures or images than through words or numbers. They also enable students to classify or categorize concepts (D) by comparing, contrasting, separating, and grouping them (C).

12. A: Younger students commonly do not yet think abstractly, and beginning and struggling students of all ages benefit from using concrete objects to understand unfamiliar abstract concepts. Having them sort objects or pictures by initial phonemes promotes phonics understanding and word-decoding skills. Rather than saying phonemes whenever students identify or discriminate them (B), teachers can prompt students to say them aloud. Rather than pointing out letters and words in environmental materials (C), having students do this is more beneficial. Rather than the common error of guessing words by initial letters (D), teachers should encourage students to sound out words.

13. B: In the reading workshop approach, the teacher models a specific cognitive skill or reading strategy for the class. The students then apply that skill or strategy in reading not assigned books (B), but books of their own choice. This choice not only enables differentiation; it moreover enables students to read books most interesting to them on their individual reading levels. Reading workshops allow both one-on-one teacher conferences with students (C) needing more help with particular skills or strategies, and time for other students to read independently (D).

14. C: The WWC recommends differentiated instruction to students in all three tiers of RTI programs. However, it recommends intensive instruction (A) only for students in Tiers 2 and 3 (20-40 minutes three to five times weekly for Tier 2, daily for Tier 3). Small-group instruction (B) is common to Tiers 2 and 3 to enable more intensive intervention; Tier 1 typically encompasses independent, paired, small-group, and whole-class instruction. While the WWC panel concedes that the ideal primary-grades classroom reading instruction would be evidence-based (D), it finds insufficient research evidence on which to base it.

15. D: In the typical structure of a guided reading lesson as an alternative structure for differentiating instruction, the teacher selects the text to read (A) by difficulty levels appropriate to the students. The teacher introduces the text to students before they begin reading (B). After students read with guidance from the teacher (e.g.; support for word decoding and identification, comprehension, meaning construction, error correction, etc.), the class discusses the text (C) meaning. In guided reading lessons, teachers also instruct students in applying specific strategies to reading activities (D).

16. C: Skills-focused lessons are effective when they maintain a faster pace (A), are interactive rather than teacher-centered (B), and target the reading skills most critical for each individual reading group (C). While small groups are most common in this lesson structure, teachers use one-on-one instruction, student pairs, and other grouping methods as well (D).

17. A: The gradual release model progresses in steps from explicit instruction to independent student work. First, in modeling and demonstration, students observe what the teacher does. Second, in teacher-led collaboration, students help what the teacher does. Third, in guided practice, students and teacher both do. Fourth, in student-led collaboration, the teacher helps what the students do. Fifth, in independent practice, the teacher observes and assesses what the students do.

18. B: LEAD21 (Wright Group, McGraw-Hill) identifies four central components of reading instruction: (1) teachers read to students, (2) teachers read with large student groups, (3) teachers read with small student groups, and (4) individual students read. Choice A represents four sizes of grouping in reading instruction. Choice C represents four types of instructional activities for reading. Choice D represents four types of grouping in reading instruction.

19. D: Among LEAD21's guiding principles for SGRI, included are the need to *differentiate* reading instruction (A), the need to focus *less* on progress as sufficient and *more* on proficiency as necessary (B), the need to inform instruction using assessment that is ongoing, not periodic (C), and the need to accelerate progress for students with the highest needs to close learning gaps (D).

20. A: In SGRI, the intensive category identifies students who read significantly below their grade level. The strategic descriptor identifies students who read below their grade level. The benchmark classification identifies students who are reading at their grade level. The advanced group identifies students who read above their grade level.

21. D: For reading instruction, flexible small groups can be created by student skill levels within a classroom or across classrooms. Grouping within the classroom is heterogeneous (A); grouping across all classrooms at one grade level is more homogeneous (B). For within-classroom groups, schools can bring in additional materials, staff, and other resources (C) during reading block times for small-group instruction. For across-classroom groups, depending on student needs, students' original classroom teacher or another teacher may give them reading instruction (D).

22. C: Various researchers have found that people spend 70 percent of waking hours communicating, and three-quarters of that time is spent listening and speaking. In total, communication time consists of 30 percent speaking, 16 percent reading, 9 percent writing, and 45 percent listening. Yet other researchers have found that schools have spent 12 years formally teaching writing, 6-8 years teaching reading, 1-2 years teaching speaking, and 0-6 months teaching listening.

23. A: Having younger students retell stories that have been read aloud to them is one way teachers can develop, practice, and demonstrate skills for listening and speaking. Another way is to have them make up their own stories and then tell them (B). Another is to use play centers to have children pretend to be story characters (C). Another way is to have children think aloud about the subject content they are learning, which reflects their thinking habits (D).

24. B: Students may be surprised to learn that only 10 percent of our communication involves words, whereas 90 percent of it involves vocal tones, facial expressions, gestures, and body language. Informing them of this statistic can help impress upon them the weight that nonverbal aspects carry in our communication, which in turn can engage their interest in developing their nonverbal communication skills.

25. A: Teachers can encourage ELLs to speak English through meaningful activities that include choral readings, which are less daunting than solo readings, give a sense of safety and strength in numbers, and provide the least proficient or confident students with multiple models or partners. Echo reading is useful (B) by modeling correct reading that students emulate. Shared reading and writing promote both understanding and use of English language, thus promoting English speech (C). Singing encourages speech (D) by providing an easier way to vocalize in English through the added structure of melody and rhythm and the ability to memorize lyrics beforehand.

26. C: In this type of ELP standard, third-grade ELLs should understand and follow one-step directions at the beginning level, two- to three-step directions at the early intermediate level, three- to four-step directions at the intermediate and early advanced level, and multiple-step directions at the advanced level (A). They should also be able to follow directions for movement in space relative to position at the beginning, early intermediate, and intermediate levels; and relative to position, frequency, and duration at the early advanced and advanced levels (B). Therefore, (D) is incorrect.

27. D: Restricted vocabulary, improper grammar patterns, and using word meanings incorrectly are symptoms of a language disorder, along with inability to follow directions, express ideas, or understand the meanings of seen or heard words, and difficulty getting others to understand intended communications, etc. Omitting, adding, substituting, or distorting phonemes (A) are symptoms of an articulation disorder. Repetitions, prolongations, and blocks (B) are symptoms of stuttering, a fluency or rate and rhythm disorder. Difficulties with loudness, pitch, or tone quality (C) are symptoms of a voice disorder. These three are all types of speech disorders.

28. B: In order to teach segmentation, i.e., separating linguistic units into their component parts, on multiple phonological levels, the educator must teach students to separate sentences (a higher level) into their component words (A) and to separate words (the next level down) into their component syllables, or into their onsets (initial phonemes) and rimes (following phoneme groups) (C). They must also teach students to separate syllables into their individual phonemes (D). Whereas choice B includes multiple phonological levels, the other choices only address one phonological level each.

29. C: Researchers have found that not all children benefit from instruction in phonological awareness (A), even though most children do. Children at risk for speech or language delays do not benefit most (B); studies providing this instruction have shown that almost one-third of at-risk children realized little or no improvement. But the benefits are not limited to children with normal language development (D), either. Some of these researchers have concluded the instruction must be more intensive or explicit for at-risk students.

30. A: According to the National Research Council (Snow, Burns, and Griffin, 1998), phonological awareness is the general ability to distinguish speech sounds from their meanings, whereas phonemic awareness is a more specific ability to distinguish individual speech sounds, i.e., phonemes, within words. Hence phonemic awareness is the most sophisticated level of phonological awareness (D). Therefore, choice B and C are also incorrect.

31. C: Instruction in phonemic awareness should be individualized to address each child's specific needs. While it is a basic skill and the main prerequisite in reading instruction, this does not mean it should be standardized across students (A), because children start school with very different levels of phonemic awareness (B). Instruction in phonemic awareness is critical because phonemic awareness strongly predicts future reading ability (D).

32. B: When creating picture flashcards to help teach children phonemic awareness, the pictures chosen should be familiar to the child (A) so he or she can name them. The child should be asked not only to name each picture with a word (C), but also, after naming it, to identify the first and second phonemes in the word (B). This helps the child understand that words contain individual sounds. This strategy is particularly helpful for children who do not have strong phonics skills (D), which involve sound-letter correspondences.

33. D: Research (cf. Inverizzi, 2003) shows that in the normal developmental sequence of phonemic awareness abilities, it is much easier for young children to identify initial phonemes (at the beginnings of words) and final phonemes (at the ends of words) than it is for them to identify medial phonemes (in the middles of words). This demonstrates the importance of systematic instruction.

34. A: When kindergarten teachers lead children in singing sight words to catchy tunes, the association of words with music is a mnemonic device that is fun and helps them remember (B) both new words and how to spell them (C). Young children generally love singing (D), making this activity entertaining as well as effective for them to learn sight words.

35. A: The distinction between vowel and consonant sounds should not be taught for the first time when teaching which letters represent which sounds, but introduced earlier, during instruction in phonemic awareness. This concept should be reviewed after teaching students to decode a small set of letter-sound matches and to recognize and form letter shapes and names.

36. B: Experts advise teachers not to advance to new letter-sound association material too quickly (A) with students who have recall or naming difficulty, because they need extensive practice or they will forget the associations they were taught before (B). Overlearning is recommended for these students (C). They should perform not only perfectly, but automatically to enable good decoding and encoding. Teachers should not focus only on new material, but combine reviewing earlier instruction with new instruction in every lesson (D).

37. C: Final blending individually identifies and pronounces each phoneme in a word before blending them. This helps teachers identify specific problem areas: some students may give the wrong sound for a letter; others may identify letter-sounds correctly without blending (e.g., pronouncing /sa/ as "suh-ah," not "sah"). Successive blending (A) pronounces individual phonemes sequentially; teachers first prolong (e.g., "ssssuuuunnnn"), then gradually shorten prolonged phonemes ("sssuuunnn," "ssuunn," "sun"). Teachers help students eventually transition from blending aloud to silent blending (B). Line blending (D) cumulatively reviews word sets and sentences already taught until students can blend independently.

38. B: Both words identified in this choice have the same medial consonant sound of /s/, whereas *kitten* has the medial consonant /t/. The two words identified in choice A have the same medial *vowel* sound. The one word identified in choice C has a different medial *vowel* sound than the other two. The two words identified in choice D have the same *final* consonant sound; the other word does not.

39. D: Research shows that phonics instruction is more effective than no phonics instruction, and also that it is more effective when it is systematic and explicit then when it is not (A). Research also shows that it is equally effective for children of all socioeconomic levels (B), that it is more effective when introduced in kindergarten or first grade (C), and that it is more effective when it helps students understand why they are learning letter-sound relationships and helps them apply this learning (D) to reading and writing.

40. A: Consonant digraphs combine two consonants to make a single sound, e.g., *ch*, *sh*, *th*, *wh*, *ck*, and ng. The word "shocking" contains three consonant digraphs: *sh-*, *-ck-*, and *-ng*. Consonant blends combine two or three consecutive consonant sounds, e.g., *bl*, *cl*, sc, *sm*, *scr*, *spl*, *spr*, *str*, etc. "Screams" (B) contains the *scr* consonant blend. "Splashes" (C) contains the *spl* consonant blend, plus the consonant digraph *sh*. "Smoking" (D) contains the consonant blend *sm*, plus the consonant digraph *-ng*.

41. C: Synthetic phonics (A) involves blending individual phonemes into words. Onsets and rimes (B) involve identifying the part of a syllable or word before the vowel (onset) and the part including and following the vowel (rime), which enables decoding many words in the same family. Structural analysis (C) involves identifying component word parts to determine meaning and pronunciation. Analytic phonics (D) involves identifying letter-sound correspondences in words already known or learned.

42. B: A phoneme (A) is an individual speech sound. A grapheme (C) is an individual written symbol, like an alphabet letter or punctuation mark. A sememe (D) is the meaning carried by a morpheme; e.g., the *-s* at the end of a noun is a morpheme; its sememe is pluralization. A morpheme (B) is the smallest individual meaningful grammatical unit that cannot be broken down further; *-tion* is thus a single morpheme, though it contains multiple phonemes and graphemes. Its sememe might be called verb nominalization.

43. A: Context skills, i.e., the strategies a student uses to acquire incidental vocabulary learning by using context clues (e.g., surrounding words, illustrations, titles, captions, etc.), represent an implicit learning strategy. The other answer choices are all explicit instructional strategies. Root analysis (B) involves identifying common Greek and Latin roots in new words to inform their meanings. Word maps (C) are graphic organizers used to identify a word's category, qualities, and examples to inform comprehension. Using keywords or word clues (e.g., images, examples, or definition parts) (D) helps students to figure out vocabulary words without needing to memorize definitions before reading.

44. D: Found within a text, a glossary is a list of key vocabulary words or technical terms used specifically in that text, along with their definitions. This will most efficiently help students find the meanings of unfamiliar terminology. Encyclopedias (A) provide extensive information about people, places, and things rather than word definitions. Dictionaries (B) give definitions of all or most words in the language, which would be less efficient for looking up words or terms specific to one text. A thesaurus (C) provides synonyms for all or most words defined in dictionaries.

45. C: Motivation, i.e., how interested students are in reading and in what ways (e.g., genres, subject matter, reading levels, etc.), is a psychological factor that influences not only whether or how much students read but also their comprehension. Attention (A) is a prerequisite for comprehension, problems with visual and auditory perception (C) can cause reading problems, and working memory (D) is required for word decoding and reading comprehension. Unlike motivation, these three are all cognitive factors.

46. A: A KWL chart is a type of graphic organizer that teachers can have students make to assist them with reading comprehension. K stands for *know*: before reading, students record what they already know about the subject of a text. W stands for *want*: before and during reading, students record what they want to know about the subject. L stands for *learned*: after reading, students record what they learned from reading the text.

47. B: Several researchers studying data from a national sample of teenagers found that high school students not only scored higher on reading achievement tests, but also got higher English grades, when their parents checked their homework (A), discussed school plans with them (B), kept high educational expectations for them (C), and discussed future plans with them (D). The researchers concluded that parental support and interest for reading and other school subjects continues to enhance academic development through the high school years.

48. A: Teacher "think-alouds" using text the students are reading reflect the explicit instruction component of modeling, i.e., the teacher demonstrates how to use a comprehension strategy. Before modeling, the teacher should use direct explanation (D) to inform students why or how a strategy aids comprehension and when to use it. After modeling, the teacher helps students learn when and how to use the strategy through guided practice (C). Then the teacher helps students practice applying it (B) until they can do so independently.

49. C: As the National Council of Teachers of English (NCTE) and International Literacy Association (ILA) point out, multiple researchers have found that the more experience students acquire with reading various literary genres, the more success they realize with writing in various genres (A). Experts find that analyzing various literary genres enables students to apply similar, not different (B), strategies and skills (e.g., identifying themes) across genres, promoting cognitive development (C). Genre studies expose students to many genres, which is more important than in-depth study of only one or two (D).

50. D: Although some history textbooks may use narrative (A) writing to make historical events more interesting by telling a story, these are not in the majority. Persuasive (B) writing seeks to convince readers to agree with the author's position; most content-area textbooks used in public schools present information more objectively. Descriptive (C) writing seeks to convey a vivid impression of something by providing sensory details so readers feel they are experiencing it; most content-area textbooks are more factual. The majority of school content textbooks use informational (D) writing to impart knowledge.

51. B: The signal words in (A) indicate a sequential, chronological text structure. The signal words in (B) indicate a descriptive text structure. The signal words in (C) indicate a comparison-contrast text structure. The signal words in (D) indicate a cause-and-effect text structure.

52. C: If the author's purpose were to inform (A), the text would present facts, explain phenomena or events, or give directions. To entertain (B), the text would contain humor, satire, adventure, suspense, horror, etc. To persuade (C), the text would present a position or point(s), support it or them with evidence, and raise and refute a counterpoint(s). To analyze (D), the text would break a subject or issue into its component parts, examine these, discuss their relationships and interactions, etc.

53. A: I-Charts or Inquiry Charts guide students to collect evidence from multiple information sources to support their ideas. While I-Charts are one type of graphic organizer, graphic organizers in general (B) organize and depict information more visually and simply; many do not involve finding or organizing information sources as I-Charts do. Journaling (C) helps students develop their own ideas rather than find or use evidence to support them. RAFT (D), i.e., Reader, Audience, Format, Topic, is a reading or writing strategy that helps students understand those four components' roles, comprehend informational text, and think creatively rather than find and use supporting evidence.

54. D: For written composition, teachers should instruct students to consider not only who their expected audience is, but also the format in which the audience will read or hear their work (A), which will inform how they write. Who the audience is affects the reading level(s), vocabulary, length, and type of writing the audience expects (D). It also affects what message each student wants to convey (B) just as much as the format does (C). They should not consider any one of these above any other, but consider all equally.

55. B: Experts observe students are often defensive when their parents critique their writing, whereas when professionals emphasize the writing process over the end-product, students report they enjoy instructor feedback (A). When teachers treat writing as a process, this encourages students to explore all possibilities in a composition before choosing closure (B). If teachers divide writing into steps, students realize greater benefits, by understanding which specific aspect of their work teacher feedback is about (C), and by developing the ability to maintain more perspective about their work by viewing writing as a series of (recursive) steps, not an indivisible whole (D).

56. D: Varying levels of explicit instruction, assigning small groups, and varying amounts of writing instruction time (A) reflects the principle of incorporating differentiated instruction. Allowing enough time for systematic writing opportunities in all content subjects as well as ELA classes (B) reflects the principle of integrating teaching writing across the curriculum. Incorporating reasons and methods for explicit writing instruction (C) reflects the principle of including rationales and methods of explicit writing instruction. Effective organization, spelling, vocabulary, syntax, etc., for different subjects (D) reflect the principle of teaching knowledge that enables more effective writing.

57. C: In the five established spelling development stages, in Stage 1 (A) children learn the difference between drawing and writing, letter formation, writing directionality, and some letter-sound correspondences, but not the alphabetic principle. In Stage 3 (B), they learn long and r-controlled vowel spelling patterns, more advanced consonant patterns, diphthongs, and other less familiar vowel patterns. In Stage 2 (C), they learn the alphabetic principle, i.e., that letters represent corresponding speech sounds, and they also learn consonant and short vowel sounds, consonant blends, and digraphs. In Stage 4 (D), they learn grammatical suffixes and rules, syllabication, and homophones.

58. A: Morphemic spelling strategies are based on how meaning influences spelling. Students learn these through learning Greek, Latin, and other root and affix derivations, adding affixes to roots, and forming abbreviations and compound words. Rule-based spelling strategies (B) include knowing that multiple spellings can exist for one phoneme, vowel and consonant interactions, and other generalizations. Phonetic spelling strategies (C), which are the easiest and should be taught first, identify a (regular) word's individual phonemes and spell it using the corresponding letters. Visual spelling strategies (D) use visual memory of spelling concepts: correct spellings look right.

59. B: Teachers should instruct typically developing students in grades K-2 in capitalizing the initial letter of the first word of every sentence in written compositions. They should teach capitalization of the initial letters of salutations and closings in letters (A), names of months and weekdays (C), and names of holidays and countries (D) to typically developing students in grades 3-5.

60. C: Many students lack understanding of connecting reading to writing on research topics (A). Teachers can help them learn to formulate research questions as the first writing step through early activities like converting assignment topics into core questions and related subordinate questions (C) to approach sources. Once students have enough practice, in later years, teachers can lead class discussions of concepts and have students formulate research questions about these (B). One graphic organizer students often find helps organize ideas and arguments are mind-maps (D), with the question central, and pro and con arguments and supporting references as branches.

61. A: Researchers find that student engagement can be deeper through integrating their practice with evaluating information sources into ongoing topic discussions; thus (B) is incorrect. Teachers should provide students with *short* passages excerpted from various resources related to the discussion topic (C). They can assign students to individual, paired, or small-group work evaluating material, which they should do using a *few, set* questions, not unlimited, open-ended ones (D), to guide their evaluations.

62. B: Having students write research questions, find sources, take notes, and make outlines (A) describes the step of independent student practice. Having students make outlines from their notes and classify information while providing them with support (B) describes the step of guided practices. Asking students how they found information and the students responding by describing all steps they took (C) relates to the step of a think check. Demonstrating identifying questions, how to find information, and categorize it (D) describes the step of teacher modeling.

63. D: During a virtual tour, teachers can have students find more information by visiting both websites and computer labs (A); locate experts in fields pertinent to classroom study, including those willing to speak directly with students (B); and not only record calls, but also connect a projector, speaker, or other sound device, enabling students to hear both ends of the teacher's conversation (C). Teachers can plan for Q&A sessions near the ends of conversations and have students direct these by asking their own questions (D).

64. C: Research has found the potential of many gifted and high-achieving students wasted when schools do not engage and challenge them sufficiently and appropriately. Studies show that 90 percent of high achievers from all income levels attend college (A); however, low-income high achievers have less likelihood of graduation. Experts advise giving high achievers less directive, more open-ended questions and assignments (B) for greater challenges, and, since abilities vary widely, they also advise letting them collaborate across classrooms and grade levels (C) to find ideal matches. Differentiating instruction is as important for high achievers as struggling students, requiring more support personnel in lower grades (D) where children cannot work independently.

65. B: To adhere to basic educational measurement principles as they apply to reading assessment, the first thing schools must do is to set goals. Second, they must adopt standards, defining what students should be able to do and know at specified levels; standards should be written to enable students to meet goals previously set. Third, they must design reading curricula enabling teachers to help students meet standards previously adopted. Fourth, they must develop assessments to measure student progress toward meeting those standards. Designing tests that measure student achievement accurately depends on this sequence.

66. C: Difficulties with decoding words (A) involve problems separating written or printed words into the phonemes their letters represent and hearing and differentiating them. Many experts regard decoding difficulty as the source of most reading problems. Comprehension difficulties (B) result from decoding difficulties (A). Retention difficulties (C) result from difficulties with both comprehension (B) and decoding (A). Thus choice D is incorrect.

67. D: If a student reads aloud without any vocal changes to identify text punctuation (A), this is a sign of difficulty with decoding words. Students often exhibit difficulties with comprehension by leaving out, glossing over, or minimizing details (B) when reading. When students insert additional words that are not already in the text (C), it is a sign that the student could be rushing through the text too quickly. Having issues with connecting ideas within a text passage (D) is a common sign of difficulty with reading retention.

68. D: Studies have found some CAI not only increases literacy skills, but also attention and interaction in students with disabilities that include autism, cerebral palsy, Down syndrome, and intellectual disability (A). Using multimedia software (e.g., Delta Messages) plus instructional scaffolding is found effective for students not performing well with conventional instruction (B). Combining CAI with the Nonverbal Reading Approach for students with co-existing severe speech disorders and physical disabilities or autism was found effective, but not necessarily more effective than teacher-only instruction or teacher-plus-CAI (C). Acquisition rates depended on individual students, showing the importance of individualizing instruction (D) for this population.

69. B: When a test's items minimize guessing by students (A) through being written clearly, this is a way of determining that the assessment is reliable, not valid (A). Tests with relatively large numbers of items (C) and tests that yield consistent scores over time (D) through repeated administrations are also likely to be reliable. Tests with items measuring the construct that the test claims to measure (B) meet the overall definition of test validity.

70. A: Researchers identify norm-referenced tests, including norm-referenced reading tests, as better for assessing abstract cognitive levels and criterion-referenced tests as better for assessing concrete cognitive levels. They also identify norm-referenced tests as better for assessing heterogeneous groups and criterion-referenced as better for homogeneous groups (B). Also, norm-referenced tests are better for assessing wider ranges of ability and criterion-referenced for narrower ability ranges (C). Finally, they identify norm-referenced tests as better for assessing wider ranges of outcomes and objectives and criterion-referenced for narrower ranges of these (D).

71. D: Although many published reading programs claim that they are based on research, experts find that few programs making this claim actually are research-based (A). Many publishers of reading programs also claim the programs balance equal amounts of explicit phonics instruction and literature-based instruction, but not all of these claims are true, either (B). These experts advise teachers NOT to believe all such claims, but rather to evaluate program instructional integrity (C) objectively themselves by applying research-based criteria (D).

72. A: According to researchers (cf. Cooper 1999, Diamond-CORE 2006), the challenges of changing teacher beliefs regarding reading instruction and initiating a new, research-based reading program arise during the first year of implementation (A). The challenges of refining that new approach, and ensuring that teachers and other staff adhere to program design and implement it consistently, arise in the second year (C). The challenge of addressing teacher "domestication" of a new reading program arises during the third year (A). These experts do not address implementation's fourth year (D); the first three are more challenging.

73. C: Experts recommend that to differentiate reading instruction, teachers encourage discussions to establish background knowledge, make material relevant to students, and deepen comprehension and retention through applying information to problems and issues, beyond memorizing facts (A). Realizing that students absorb different information from lessons and demonstrations and cannot write about anything not absorbed, teachers can read student journals to assess for inferential thinking and text "chunk" analysis to inform intervention plans before assigning writing (B). Teachers should model how to construct meaning from text during multiple activity formats (C); and plan units first to understand what they want students to learn about reading strategies, genres, and issues, and ensure they collect the appropriate materials (D).

74. B: Designing a K-12 reading curriculum requires systematic planning, but NOT following a series of steps in rigid order (A). Design pursues optimal functionality, not perfection; despite all efforts to plan systematically and think inventively, compromises among everyone's wishes are inevitable (B). Decisions made at different stages are NOT independent, but interact (C); hence, the design process is often recursive. Though educators may revisit different stages, to make the design process work, they must recognize each stage's challenges and tasks. The first stage is setting design specifications; stages of conceptualizing, developing, and refining the design follow (D).

75. D: The best way for teachers to promote language, literacy, and reading development is to integrate oral language, written language, modeling, and interaction into classroom activities in a variety of interactive settings. Choices A, B, and C all call upon one aspect, but do not include any interactive steps. Choice D is the best option because it calls upon interaction and includes reading and writing, as well as the potential for oral language skills.

76. A: The NEA recommends effective school-family-community partnership strategies, including taking time to build one-to-one, learning-related family-educator relationships and discuss and agree on how best to collaborate for student success. Another is setting, communicating, and supporting high, rigorous expectations, particularly for at-risk and marginal students (B), and giving them needed support for succeeding. Another is providing support for faculty and other professionals to overcome cultural, linguistic, and class barriers, rather than just requiring that they do so (C). Establishing student-community connections not only gives students relevant, hands-on learning, but also demonstrates student and school community service (D).

77. C: Researchers (Henderson and Mapp, 2002) reviewing the literature found that when middle school and high school students' families remained involved in their educations, they made transitions to new schools better than others (A), maintained their work quality (B), made more realistic plans for the future (C), and were less likely to drop out of school than others (D).

78. D: The NEA recommends that to promote research-based strategies for developing family-school-community partnerships at the national level, school reform initiatives should put these partnerships at their centers; that not only policy forums, conferences, and comments on federal regulations, but also policy and legislative proposals, should provide for such partnerships (A); that advocacy for these partnerships in federal legislation is appropriate (B); and that NEA members should disseminate its recommended partnership strategies throughout the Association's membership (C).

79. A: The Every Student Succeeds Act (ESSA) entitles all students to equitable access to learning opportunities. For ELLs, this entails receiving appropriate linguistic supports and services to promote academic achievement and English language acquisition. While specific regulations for linguistic supports vary among states, they typically must be aligned with students' proficiency level and facilitate their full inclusion in the learning process. Therefore, Mr. Rivera has the legal and professional responsibility to give his new students linguistic accommodations that enable their full participation in learning while promoting English language proficiency development.

80. C: Team building (A) can be viewed as a type of group negotiation that can resolve conflicts and build consensus. Principled negotiation (B) is a type of bargaining based on moral, ethical, educational, organizational, or other principles for efficiently, judiciously, and respectfully reaching agreement. Conflict transformation (D) enables understanding conflict situations and changing them from destructive to productive. Positional negotiation (C) is a type of bargaining based on a negotiator's non-neutral position regarding an issue, and thus a less productive way of addressing conflict.

Constructed Response

1. Essay question graders commonly look for the following elements in a strong response: strong content knowledge, clear organization, and effective arguments or examples. Language and usage are not usually strictly graded, but they can make a big impact on the clarity of your ideas.

Please use the provided rubric to make sure your response meets these common criteria. Try to have a friend or family member grade your response for you or take a break after writing your response and return to grade it with fresh eyes.

CONSTRUCTED RESPONSE RUBRIC

Domain	Description
Content Knowledge	• The response directly addresses every part of the prompt. • The response demonstrates independent knowledge of the topic. • The response discusses the topic at an appropriate depth.
Organization	• The response introduces the topic, usually with a thesis statement or by restating the prompt. • The response directly addresses the prompt by providing a clear and concise answer or solution. • The answer or solution is supported by logical arguments or evidence. • The response restates the main idea in the conclusion.
Arguments and Examples	• The response provides a reasonable answer to the prompt. • The answer is supported by strong reasoning or evidence. • The response develops ideas logically and connects ideas to one another. • The reasoning and evidence provided act to support a unified main idea.
Language and Usage	• The response demonstrates effective use of grammar and uses varied sentence structure throughout the response. • The response demonstrates correct use of spelling, punctuation, and capitalization. • The response demonstrates strong and varied use of vocabulary relevant to the topic and appropriate for the intended audience.

2. Essay question graders commonly look for the following elements in a strong response: strong content knowledge, clear organization, and effective arguments or examples. Language and usage are not usually strictly graded, but they can make a big impact on the clarity of your ideas.

Please use the provided rubric to make sure your response meets these common criteria. Try to have a friend or family member grade your response for you or take a break after writing your response and return to grade it with fresh eyes.

Constructed Response Rubric

Domain	Description
Content Knowledge	• The response directly addresses every part of the prompt. • The response demonstrates independent knowledge of the topic. • The response discusses the topic at an appropriate depth.
Organization	• The response introduces the topic, usually with a thesis statement or by restating the prompt. • The response directly addresses the prompt by providing a clear and concise answer or solution. • The answer or solution is supported by logical arguments or evidence. • The response restates the main idea in the conclusion.
Arguments and Examples	• The response provides a reasonable answer to the prompt. • The answer is supported by strong reasoning or evidence. • The response develops ideas logically and connects ideas to one another. • The reasoning and evidence provided act to support a unified main idea.
Language and Usage	• The response demonstrates effective use of grammar and uses varied sentence structure throughout the response. • The response demonstrates correct use of spelling, punctuation, and capitalization. • The response demonstrates strong and varied use of vocabulary relevant to the topic and appropriate for the intended audience.